Tegus

Tegus as Pets

Tegu Care, Behavior, Diet, Interaction, Costs and Health.

By

Ben Team

ALL RIGHTS RESERVED. This book contains material protected under International and Federal Copyright Laws and Treaties.

Any unauthorized reprint or use of this material is strictly prohibited. No part of this book may be reproduced or transmitted in any form or by any means, electronic, mechanical or otherwise, including photocopying or recording, or by any information storage and retrieval system without express written permission from the author.

Copyrighted © 2017

Published by: Pesa Publishing

Table of Contents

Tegus 1

Table of Contents 3

About the Author 5

Foreword 6

PART I: THE TEGU 9

Chapter 1: Tegu Description and Anatomy 10

Chapter 2: Tegu Biology and Behavior 15

Chapter 3: Classification and Taxonomy 18

Chapter 4: The Tegu's World 20

PART II: TEGU HUSBANDRY 24

Chapter 5: Tegus as Pets 25

Chapter 6: Providing the Captive Habitat 37

Chapter 7: Establishing the Thermal Environment 40

Chapter 8: Lighting the Enclosure 51

Chapter 9: Substrate and Furniture 55

Chapter 10: Maintaining the Captive Habitat 63

Chapter 11: Feeding Tegus 70

Chapter 12: Providing Water to Your Tegu 76

Chapter 13: Interacting with Your Tegu 78

Chapter 14: Common Health Concerns 81

Chapter 15: Breeding Tegus 88

Chapter 16: Further Reading 92

References 97

Index 98

About the Author

The author, Ben Team, is an environmental educator and author with over 16 years of professional reptile-keeping experience.

Ben currently maintains www.FootstepsInTheForest.com, where he shares information, narration and observations of the natural world.

Foreword

Those who are interested in keeping a reptile as a pet have a number of species from which they can choose. And because each species presents a different suite of traits and characteristics, it is important to consider your choice carefully before adding a new animal to your home.

Among other things, you must consider the food habits, environmental needs and temperament of the various species you are considering. You'll also have to consider your personal, subjective preferences, the availability of the species you like and, of course, the costs associated with the animals and their care.

But one of the most important factors would-be reptile owners must consider when selecting a new pet is the size of the animal. Your new pet's size will prove to be one of the most influential characteristics, and it will alter the way in which you house, handle and feed it.

The common reptile species in the pet trade exhibit quite a bit of diversity in this regard. Leopard geckos and many other lizards measure only a few inches in length, while some snakes and turtles weigh hundreds of pounds.

Animals at both ends of this spectrum present their own challenges. The challenges presented by large reptiles are fairly obvious: They'll require more space, they'll need more food and, in some cases, they represent a greater danger.

However, animals at the small end of the spectrum present challenges to the keeper as well. For example, it can be difficult to obtain food small enough for tiny lizards and snakes. Additionally, very small critters are more fragile than their larger counterparts, which complicates handling and veterinary care.

Fortunately, there are a number of reptile species that reach moderate sizes. These animals are small enough that they aren't particularly difficult to house, nor do they represent a serious threat to life or limb. However, they are large enough that they are not especially fragile and they can easily ingest most commonly available foods.

One of the best examples of a reptile in this size class, which also makes a good pet for other reasons, is the tegu.

Tegus are medium-sized lizards hailing from South America. They reach lengths of between about 2 and 4 feet (60 to 120 centimeters) – half of which is tail. This means that they are big enough to avoid the challenges presented by tiny lizards, yet they are not large enough to require ridiculous amounts of space or food.

Although they can certainly deliver a painful bite to careless keepers, they don't represent any more danger than a large iguana or macaw does, and many tegus become quite tame anyway. They are often amenable to handling and interaction with their keeper, and their moderate size makes them enjoyable to handle.

But aside from their nearly ideal size, which appeals to many keepers, tegus also exhibit a number of other traits that make them well-suited for captivity.

For example, tegus are omnivores, who can survive on a varied diet. This provides keepers with additional flexibility. They are also remarkably hardy animals, who often withstand the indignities of captive life better than many other reptiles do.

But it is their incredible beauty that draws many to these lizards in the first place. There are several different tegu species available in the pet trade, and though each is clad in different colors and slightly different patterns, they are all gorgeous. Additionally, their smooth and supple skin is quite impressive to the touch (a fact which has unfortunately made the tegu a common species harvested for the international leather trade).

This is not to suggest that tegus are perfect pets for all keepers, as they do present several challenges. However, because size should be one of the first things prospective keepers consider when selecting a pet, tegus should usually jump to the top of the list.

As is necessary when keeping any reptile, you must familiarize yourself with the biology, natural history, personality and habits of tegus before deciding that they are the species for you. Only by doing so will you have a good chance at maintaining your lizard successfully and giving your new pet a high quality of life.

PART I: THE TEGU

Properly caring for any animal requires an understanding of the species and its place in the natural world. This includes digesting subjects as disparate as anatomy and ecology, diet and geography, and reproduction and physiology.

It is only by learning what your pet is, how it lives, what it does that you can achieve the primary goal of animal husbandry: Providing your pet with the highest quality of life possible.

Chapter 1: Tegu Description and Anatomy

Tegus are beautiful, boldly marked, medium-sized lizards. Although they share the same basic body plan as most other lizards, they are easy to identify on sight, once you become familiar with their physical characteristics.

Size

The different tegu species exhibit small size differences, but most hatch at about 8-inches (20 centimeters) in total length. They grow quickly, and most reach their full adult size over about 12 to 36 months' time.

Upon reaching maturity, most tegus are between 30 and 48 inches (75 to 120 centimeters) in total body length, of which roughly half is comprised of the tail. Males reach slightly longer lengths than females do, and they often exhibit a thicker build.

Adults can weigh as much as 15 pounds (6.8 kilograms), although most remain slightly smaller than this. Overweight specimens (which are unfortunately common in captivity) may exceed this weight slightly.

Color and Pattern

Tegus exhibit a fair degree of variation in color and pattern among different species and populations, as well as among individuals.

Most are clad in a similar pattern, featuring a dark ground color, on top of which lies white, off-white or gold spots and markings. The light-colored markings often take the form of bars or bands across the back, and many have a dotted line extending down each of their sides. Various spots and stripes are found on the legs, and the head is often heavily marked with the lighter color element.

The dark ground color of most tegus is black or very dark brown. However, red tegus (*Salvator rufescens*) have a reddish wash to their entire color scheme and some tegus (which perhaps represent a unique species or population) have a blueish ground color.

Hatchlings generally resemble the adults, except that hatchling Argentine black and white tegus (*Salvator merianae*) have green heads. The green color begins to fade shortly after hatching.

The Tegu Head

Tegus have large, impressive, triangular heads and thick, muscular necks. Well-developed eyes sit on the sides of the head. Some tegu species (those belonging to the genus *Salvator*) have round pupils, while those of others (members of the genus *Tupinambis*) have reniform (kidney-shaped) pupils. The iris is relatively large, and its color varies from gold to red to dark brown. Despite the fact that their eyes are located on the sides of their head, tegus are able to see directly forward, as their noses taper sharply.

Tegus have membrane-covered ear openings, located right behind their mouths. The membrane – called tympanums (ear drums) -- are easily seen when looking at the side of the lizard's head. Despite the small size of their ears, tegus have a good sense of hearing. Tegus have two nostrils, which are located near the front of the snout.

Mature males often develop heavy jowls, which are easy to spot. These jowls can help determine the sex of mature animals.

Note the teeth visible in this tegu's mouth.

Mouth, Tongue and Teeth

Tegus have relatively large mouths that extend well past the eyes. They have heterodont dentition, meaning that they have different types of teeth, which have evolved to play different roles. The front teeth are incisor-like, and right behind them sit the canine-like teeth. Another set of incisor-like teeth occur behind the canines, and a set of broad, molar-like teeth reside in the back of the mouth. Tegus have about 70 teeth in total.

Tegus have long, bifurcated (twin-tipped) tongues that resemble those of snakes and monitor lizards. Unlike many other lizards, who use their tongues to manipulate or capture food, tegus primarily use their tongues as sensory organs. They frequently extend their tongues when exploring or hunting, in order to learn more about their environment.

Limbs and Feet

Tegus have four very strong limbs, each of which extends laterally from the body. This arrangement allows the lizards to move effectively while climbing on tree trunks, scurrying across the ground or tunneling in the dirt. Some research indicates that tegus have unusually strong limb bones, which may be an adaptation to their burrowing habits. (K. Megan Sheffield, 2011)

Tegus have four well-developed feet, each of which bears five toes. Tegus have formidable claws, which help them to climb, dig and defend themselves from predators.

Vent

Tegus have a small opening – called the vent – on their ventral surface, near the base of the tail. The vent leads directly to the cloaca, and serves as the final exit point for waste, urates and eggs. When lizards defecate, release urates or copulate, the vent opens slightly.

Tail

Tegus have long, whip-like tails that help them keep their balance and maneuver more effectively through the dense foliage of their natural habitat. They do not appear to use their tails for any defensive purpose, as monitor lizards (with whom tegus are often compared) do.

Tegus occasionally lose portions of their tails to predators or accidents, but they do not regenerate in the way that the tails of many other lizards do.

Internal Organs

The internal anatomy of tegus differs relatively little from that of other lizards or tetrapods in general.

Tegus draw oxygen in through their nostrils; pipe it through the trachea and into the lungs. Here, blood exchanges carbon dioxide for oxygen, before it is pumped to the various body parts via the heart and blood vessels.

While the tegu's heart features only three true chambers (two atria and a single ventricle), a septum keeps the ventricle divided at most times, allowing the heart to operate similarly to a four-chambered, mammalian heart. This means that in practice, tegus keep their oxygenated and deoxygenated blood relatively separate in the heart.

Their digestive system is comprised of an esophagus, stomach, small intestine, large intestine and a terminal chamber called the cloaca. The stomach has some ability to stretch to accommodate food.

The liver resides near the center of the animal's torso, with the gall bladder sitting directly behind it. While the gall bladder stores bile, the liver provides a number of functions relating to digestion, metabolism and filtration. Kidneys, which lie almost directly behind the lungs, filter wastes from the lizard's bloodstream.

Like all other lizards, tegus control their bodies via their brain and nervous system. Their endocrine and exocrine glands work much as they do in other vertebrates.

Reproductive Organs

Like all squamates, male tegus have paired reproductive organs, called hemipenes. When not in use, males keep their hemipenes inside the bases of their tails. When they attempt to mate with a female, they evert one of the hemipenes and insert it into the female's cloaca.

The paired nature of the male sex organs ensures that males can continue to breed if they suffer injury to one of the hemipenes. This paired arrangement also allows male tegus to mate with females on either side of their body.

Females have paired ovaries, which produce ova (eggs), and they have paired oviducts, which store the eggs after they are released from the ovaries.

The eggs are shelled and held inside the oviducts until it is time to deposit the eggs. At this time, the eggs are passed from the oviducts into the cloaca and out of the body via the vent.

Chapter 2: Tegu Biology and Behavior

Tegus exhibit a number of biological and behavioral adaptations that allow them to survive in their natural habitats. It is important to familiarize yourself with these adaptations, so that you can provide the best possible care for your new pet.

Shedding

Like other scaled reptiles, tegus shed their old skin to reveal new, fresh skin underneath. However, they do not always shed their skin in one piece, as most snakes do, instead, they often allow the skin to break into a few, large pieces.

Sometimes, tegus consume their shed skin, in order to recover any nutrients present in the old, dead cells.

Metabolism and Digestion

Tegus are ectothermic ("cold-blooded") animals, whose internal metabolism depends on the lizard's body temperature. When they are warm, their bodily functions proceed more rapidly; but when they are cold, their bodily functions proceed slowly.

This also means that tegus digest more effectively at suitably warm temperatures than they do at suboptimal temperatures. Their appetites also vary with temperature, and if the temperatures drop below the preferred range, they may cease feeding entirely.

A lizard's body temperature largely follows ambient air temperatures, but it also absorbs and reflects radiant heat, such as that coming from the sun. The lizards try to keep their body temperature within the preferred range by employing behaviors that allow them to adjust their temperature.

For example, tegus may bask to warm their temperature when they are too cool. This typically involves orienting their body so that they are perpendicular with the sun's rays. Some individuals may exhibit darker colors when basking to help absorb more infrared rays.

By contrast, when it is necessary to cool off, tegus may move into the shade or retreat into a burrow to lower their body temperature.

Growth Rate and Lifespan
After completing their incubation period, tegus hatch from their eggs. They grow quickly, and most wild specimens probably reach maturity in about 12 to 36 months.

Most wild-living tegus probably die within their first few years of life – much like most other lizard species. However, those that reach adulthood probably live relatively long lives.

Many individuals live for more than 10 years, and captives can live for longer than this, thanks in part to the fact that captive individuals needn't cope with predators or food shortages. The maximum age for tegus is probably about 15 to 20 years.

Foraging Behavior
Tegus are actively foraging predators, who search far and wide for food. Most (particularly young or small individuals) feed heavily on invertebrates, but large individuals will also consume small lizards, rodents, amphibians and birds. The eggs of birds, turtles, snakes and other lizards are also an important food source. Tegus also opportunistically feed on some fruits and plant material, and some individuals appear to forage in parks and other areas, where they feed on food dropped or left by humans.

When a tegu sees a suitable prey item, they quickly pounce on it and grab the animal with their mouth. They usually squeeze down on the prey item several times with their strong jaws to incapacitate it, and then they proceed to swallow it.

Diel and Seasonal Activity
Tegus are almost exclusively diurnal, meaning they are active during the day and sleep through the night. They typically rise shortly after sunrise and remain active for a few hours before settling back in to their hiding place to escape the mid-day heat. Some may also become active in the afternoon.

In the southern portions of their range, tegus may brumate (hibernate) during the cold winter. In some cases, this brumation period may last for 5 to 7 months. Mating usually commences shortly after tegus emerge from hibernation for southern species, but it can occur at any time of the year for those living in the hot and humid northern reaches of South America.

Most females deposit a clutch of eggs after the first breeding cycle, and many will deposit a second clutch in the late summer or early fall.

Defensive Strategies and Tactics

Tegus are cryptic animals that blend well with their environment. This helps them to avoid detection by most would-be predators, such as hawks, large cats and humans.

Tegus usually attempt to flee from predators that see through their camouflaged patterns, but some may face adversaries and gape their mouths or bite – this is particularly common among the larger individuals.

Tegus may also defecate or release urates when grasped by a predator (or their keeper).

Reproduction

Males and females may breed with several different individuals over the course of the breeding season, and there is some evidence that females who are bred by more than one male produce clutches with higher fertility rates than those who only breed a single male.

Females often construct a primitive nest in which they'll deposit their eggs. Egg- and nest-guarding behavior are quite common and very effective. Some females may retain the sperm from a single mating and deposit a second clutch of eggs a few months after depositing their first.

Chapter 3: Classification and Taxonomy

Tegus are a well-defined group of lizards, who likely spring from a common ancestor. While their taxonomy has been subject to several revisions, most researchers agree that this group of lizards represents a single clade.

But before delving more deeply into the classification and taxonomy of tegus, it is helpful to begin with a broader context.

Although the taxonomy of lizards is the subject of great debate, the Integrated Taxonomic Information System currently classifies all of the living tegus in the the order Squamata and the suborder Autarchoglossa.

Autarchoglossa, as presently construed, contains 13 different families, including Anguidae, Anniellidae, Cordylidae, Gerrhosauridae, Gymnophthlamidae, Helodermatidae, Lacertidae, Lanthanotidae, Scincidae, Varanidae, Xantusiidae, Xenosauridae and Teiidae, which contains all of the living tegu species

The family Teiidae contains a number of different genera, including *Ameiva*, *Callopistes*, *Cnemidophorus*, *Crocodilurus*, *Dicrodon*, *Dracaena*, *Kentropyx*, *Teius* and *Tupinambis*, which, until recently contained all of the living tegu species.

However, recent workers have split the living tegus into two different genera: *Tupinambis* and *Salvator*.

Generally speaking, the species hailing from the southern reaches of South America are placed in the genus *Salvator*, while those at the northern reaches of South America are members of the genus *Tupinambis*.

Within these two genera, scientists who subscribe to the two-genus classification scheme recognize seven species:

- Gold tegu (*Tupinambis teguixin*)

- Rhondonia tegu (*Tupinambis longilineus*)

- Swamp tegu (*Tupinambis palustris*)

- Four-lined tegu (*Tupinambis quadrilineatus*)

- Argentine Black and White Tegu (*Salvator merianae*)

- Red tegu (*Salvator rufescens*)

- Yellow tegu (*Salvator duseni*)

However, recent work suggests that the gold tegu is actually a combination of three different species. All three species are essentially identical to the human eye, and they may even be sympatric (occupying the same range). (John C. Murphy, 2016)

More research will be necessary to further clarify our understanding of the systematics of the tegus.

Chapter 4: The Tegu's World

To maintain a tegu successfully, you must understand the animal's native habitat and provide a reasonable facsimile of it.

Range
Although there are feral populations in Florida, tegus are native to South America and the southernmost portions of Central America. They are restricted to the eastern portion of the continent, and do not cross the Andes.

Although the individual species have varying ranges, the entire group ranges from Panama to Argentina. Because much of this range is poorly known, the exact distributions of the various species remain unclear.

Climate
Generally speaking, tegus live in areas with warm to hot summers and mild to cool winters. Rainfall varies significantly across their range, with those living in the northern portions of South America enjoying ample, year-round rainfall and those in the south experiencing rain only during a relatively brief portion of the year.

Freezing temperatures rarely occur in the tropical portions of South America, but they occur regularly in the southern reaches of these lizards' range.

Habitat
Tegus are very adaptable lizards, and they live in a number of different habitats across their range. This includes rainforests, near deserts, savannahs, open forests and riparian areas, as well as every habitat in between these. They can also live in suburban areas and parklands, and those who've been introduced to Florida inhabit a variety of forests and hammocks.

Status in the Wild
Because of the lack of clarity regarding the taxonomic status of the various tegu species, the status of wild populations is difficult to ascertain. Indeed, the exact ranges of many tegu species are poorly

understood, so it is obviously difficult to determine their wild populations.

The IUCN Redlist of Threatened Species only assesses the population level of one tegu species (*Salvator merianae*), which it categorizes as being of "Least Concern." This indicates that the population appears to be healthy.

Tegus are harvested extensively in many countries for their hides, which are turned into leather boots, bags and belts. However, several countries impose strict quota systems, which are intended to prevent the overharvest of this resource.

Natural Diet

Relatively little research has been conducted on the feeding habits of the wild-living tegu species, so the specific food items they prefer remain unknown except for a handful of lizards that have been studied scientifically.

However, it is quite clear that tegus have very broad and flexible diets. They likely consume the foods that are most readily available in their local habitat. The diet of these lizards changes as they age – a phenomenon known as an ontogenetic dietary shift. This occurs alongside a change in dentition that occurs with age: Young tegus have only sharp, pointy teeth, which are ideally suited for catching small prey, while the adults have molar-like teeth, which are better adapted for plant matter.

Insects and other invertebrates are important dietary staples, although juveniles probably eat more insects and invertebrates than adults do. Many of the insect types that are especially important include beetles (and their larvae) and orthopterans (grasshoppers, crickets and their kin). Roaches play an important role in their diet as well.

Several vertebrates also figure prominently into the diet of tegus. Even small tegus may consume other lizards or tiny snakes, but adults can consume lizards and snakes of relatively impressive size. Amphibians, rodents and birds are also eaten when the chance arises, and while fish are unlikely to make up a substantial portion of their diets, it seems unlikely that tegus would pass up the opportunity to consume them when available.

Tegus also eat a lot of vegetation, especially fruits. Because they often consume fruits wholly, they serve as important agents of seed dispersal. Few studies have specifically examined the fruits and vegetables consumed, but they are known to eat bananas, figs and palm fruits.

Tegus are usually willing to take advantage of any novel food source that presents itself, including everything from carrion to human refuse.

Natural Predators

Hatchling and juvenile tegus are – like most other small lizards – at risk of predation by a variety of small and medium-sized predators. This includes everything from snakes to birds to small primates. Most juveniles try to remain hidden as much as is possible to avoid these threats.

An Argentine black and white tegu.

Although adult tegus are robust lizards, who are quite capable of defending themselves, they are occasionally consumed by other animals. In fact, virtually every large or medium-sized predator that shares habitat with tegus represents a potential threat.

Some of the most important predators adult tegus must avoid include large snakes, such as boa constrictors (Boa constrictor spp.), and large birds of prey. Predatory cats also prey on these lizards from time to time, as does the occasional crocodilian.

Nevertheless, humans are probably one of the most important predators of adult tegus. People hunt tegus for the meat they provide, as well as their hides.

PART II: TEGU HUSBANDRY

Once equipped with a basic understanding of what tegus *are* (Chapter 1 and Chapter 3), where they *live* (Chapter 4), and what they *do* (Chapter 2) you can begin learning about their captive care.

Animal husbandry is an evolving pursuit. Keepers shift their strategies frequently as they incorporate new information and ideas into their husbandry paradigms.

There are few "right" or "wrong" answers, and what works in one situation may not work in another. Accordingly, you may find that different authorities present different, and sometimes conflicting, information regarding the care of these lizards.

In all cases, you must strive to learn as much as you can about your pet and its natural habitat, so that you may provide it with the best quality of life possible.

Chapter 5: Tegus as Pets

Tegus can make rewarding pets, but you must know what to expect before adding one to your home and family. This includes not only understanding the nature of the care they require, but also the costs associated with this care.

Assuming that you feel confident in your ability to care for a lizard and endure the associated financial burdens, you can begin seeking your individual pet.

Understanding the Commitment
Keeping a tegu as a pet requires a substantial commitment. You will be responsible for your pet's well-being for the rest of its life. Tegus are long-live animals, and you must be prepared to care for your new pet for many years.

Can you be sure that you will still want to care for your pet several years in the future? Do you know what your living situation will be? What changes will have occurred in your family? How will your working life have changed over this time?

You must consider all of these possibilities before acquiring a new pet. Failing to do so often leads to apathy, neglect and even resentment, which is not good for you or your pet lizard.

Neglecting your pet is wrong, and in some locations, a criminal offense. You must continue to provide quality care for your tegu, even once the novelty has worn off, and it is no longer fun to clean the cage and purchase crickets a few times a week.

Once you purchase a tegu, its well-being becomes your responsibility until it passes away at the end of a long life, or you have found someone who will agree to adopt the animal for you. Unfortunately, this is rarely an easy task. You may begin with thoughts of selling your pet to help recoup a small part of your investment, but these efforts will largely fall flat.

While professional breeders may profit from the sale of tegus, amateurs are at a decided disadvantage. Only a tiny sliver of the general population is interested in reptilian pets, and only a small subset of these are interested in keeping tegus.

Of those who are interested in acquiring a tegu, most would rather start fresh, by *purchasing* a small hatchling or juvenile from an established breeder, rather than adopting your questionable animal *for free*.

After having difficulty finding a willing party to purchase or adopt your animal, many owners try to donate their pet to a local zoo. Unfortunately, this rarely works either.

Zoos are not interested in your tegu, no matter how pretty or tame he is. He is a pet with little to no reliable provenance and questionable health status. This is simply not the type of animal zoos are eager to add to their multi-million dollar collections.

Zoos obtain most of their animals from other zoos and museums; failing that, they obtain their animals directly from their land of origin. As a rule, they do not accept donated pets.

No matter how difficult it becomes to find a new home for your unwanted lizard, you must never release non-native reptiles into the wild. Tegus can colonize places outside their native range (and they have done exactly this is several locations), with disastrous results for the ecosystem's native fauna.

Additionally, released or escaped reptiles cause a great deal of distress to those who are frightened by them. This leads local municipalities to adopt pet restrictions or ban reptile keeping entirely.

While the chances of an escaped or released tegu harming anyone are very low, it is unlikely that those who fear reptiles will see the threat as minor.

The Costs of Captivity
Reptiles are often marketed as low-cost pets. While true in a relative sense (the costs associated with dog, cat, horse or tropical fish husbandry are often much higher than they are for tegus), potential keepers must still prepare for the financial implications of tegu ownership.

At the outset, you must budget for the acquisition of your pet, as well as the costs of purchasing or constructing a habitat. Unfortunately, while many keepers plan for these costs, they typically fail to consider the on-going costs, which will quickly eclipse the initial startup costs.

Startup Costs

One surprising fact most new keepers learn is the enclosure and equipment will often cost as much as (or more than) the animal does (except in the case of very high-priced specimens).

Prices fluctuate from one market to the next, but in general, the least you will spend on a healthy tegu is about $50 (£40), while the least you will spend on the *initial* habitat and assorted equipment will be about $50 (£40). Replacement equipment and food will represent additional (and ongoing) expenses.

Examine the charts on the following pages to get an idea of three different pricing scenarios. While the specific prices listed will vary based on innumerable factors, the charts are instructive for first-time buyers.

The first scenario details a budget-minded keeper, trying to spend as little as possible. The second example estimates the costs for a keeper with a moderate budget, and the third example provides a case study for extravagant shoppers, who want an expensive tegu and top-notch equipment.

These charts are only provided estimates; your experience may vary based on a variety of factors.

Inexpensive Option

Wild Caught Gold Tegu	$50 (£38)
Economy Homemade Habitat	$50 (£38)
Heat Lamp Fixture and Bulbs	$20 (£15)
Plants, Substrate, Hides, etc.	$20 (£15)
Infrared Thermometer	$35 (£27)
Digital Indoor-Outdoor Thermometer	$20 (£15)
Water Dish, Forceps, Spray Bottles, Misc.	$20 (£15)
Total	$215 (£163)

Moderate Option

Captive Bred Argentine Black and White Tegu	$150 (£115)
Premium Homemade Habitat	$100 (£76)
Heat Lamp Fixture and Bulbs	$20 (£16)
Plants, Substrate, Hides, etc.	$20 (£16)
Infrared Thermometer	$35 (£27)
Digital Indoor-Outdoor Thermometer	$20 (£16)
Water Dish, Forceps, Spray Bottles, Misc.	$20 (£16)
Total	$240 (£191)

Premium Option

Captive Bred Adult Red Tegu	$400 (£306)
Premium Commercial Cage	$500 (£383)
Heat Lamp Fixture and Bulbs	$20 (£15)
Plants, Substrate, Hides, etc.	$20 (£15)
Infrared Thermometer	$35 (£27)
Digital Indoor-Outdoor Thermometer	$20 (£15)
Water Dish, Forceps, Spray Bottles, Misc.	$20 (£15)
Total	$1,015 (£776)

Ongoing Costs

The ongoing costs of tegu ownership primarily fall into one of three categories: food, maintenance and veterinary care.

Food costs are the most significant of the three, but they are relatively consistent and somewhat predictable. Some maintenance costs are easy to calculate, but things like equipment malfunctions are impossible to predict with any certainty. Veterinary expenses are hard to predict and vary wildly from one year to the next.

Food Costs

Food is the single greatest ongoing cost you will experience while caring for your tegu. To obtain a reasonable estimate of your yearly food costs, you must consider the number of meals you will feed your pet per year and the cost of each meal.

The amount of food your lizard will consume will vary based on numerous factors, including his size, the average temperatures in his habitat and his health.

As a ballpark number, you should figure that you'll need about $10 (£8) per week – roughly $500 (£383) per year -- for food. You could certainly spend more or less than this, but that is a reasonable estimate for back-of-the-envelope calculations.

Veterinary Costs

While you should always seek veterinary advice at the first sign of illness, it is probably not wise to haul your healthy tegu to the vet's office for no reason – they don't require "checkups" or annual vaccinations as some other pets may. Accordingly, you shouldn't incur any veterinary expenses unless your pet falls ill.

However, veterinary care can become very expensive, very quickly. In addition to a basic exam or phone consultation, your lizard may need cultures, x-rays or other diagnostic tests performed. In light of this, wise keepers budget at least $200 to $300 (£160 to £245) each year to cover any emergency veterinary costs.

Maintenance Costs

It is important to plan for both routine and unexpected maintenance costs. Commonly used items, such as paper towels, disinfectant and top soil are rather easy to calculate. However, it is not easy to know how many burned out light bulbs, cracked misting units or faulty thermostats you will have to replace in a given year.

Those who keep their tegu in simple enclosures will find that about $50 (£40) covers their yearly maintenance costs. By contrast, those who maintain elaborate habitats may spend $200 (£160) or more each year.

Always try to purchase frequently used supplies, such as light bulbs, paper towels and disinfectants in bulk to maximize your savings. It is often beneficial to consult with local reptile-keeping clubs, who often pool their resources to attain greater buying power.

Myths and Misunderstandings

Myth: Tegus need "friends" or they will get lonely.

Fact: Although they can occasionally be kept in small groups, consisting of two or three females and a single male, without problem, tegus are essentially solitary animals in the wild, who spend the bulk of their lives alone. Accordingly, they will never "miss" having cagemates, and you should not feel obligated to keep them in a communal setting.

Myth: Reptiles grow in proportion to the size of their cage and then stop.

Fact: Reptiles do no such thing. Most healthy lizards, snakes and turtles grow throughout their lives, although the rate of growth slows with age (a very few stop growing with maturity, although this is not influenced by the size of their cage).

Placing them in a small cage in an attempt to stunt their growth is an unthinkably cruel practice, which is more likely to sicken or kill your pet than stunt its growth.

Myth: Tegus must eat live food.

Fact: Most tegus will accept live or pre-killed prey. However, it may be necessary to "animate" dead food items by moving them around with a pair of tongs. Additionally, most tegus will eat small amounts of plant material (particularly fruits).

Myth: Reptiles have no emotions and do not suffer.

Fact: While tegus have very primitive brains and do not have emotions comparable to those of higher mammals, they can absolutely suffer. Always treat reptiles with the same compassion you would offer a dog, cat or horse.

Myth: Tegus are vicious lizards that bite at every chance.

Fact: While some tegus are often defensive, many calm down and learn to accept brief interactions with their keeper. This is most common among captive bred offspring; wild caught adults rarely tolerate being touched by their keeper.

Myth: Tegus prefer elaborately decorated cages that resemble their natural habitat.

Fact: While most lizards do thrive better in complex habitats that offer a variety of hiding and thermoregulatory options, they do not appreciate your aesthetic efforts. Additionally, the foraging activity of your tegu will likely destroy any decorations you incorporate.

Additionally, while tegus require hiding spaces, they do not seem to mind whether this hiding space is in the form of a rock, a rotten log or piece of lumber. As long as the hiding spot is safe and snug, they will utilize it.

Acquiring Your Tegu

Modern reptile enthusiasts can acquire tegus from a variety of sources, each with a different set of pros and cons.

Pet stores are one of the first places many people see tegus, and they become the de facto source of pets for many beginning keepers. While they do offer some unique benefits to prospective keepers, pet stores are not always the best place to purchase a lizard; so, consider all of the available options, including breeders and reptile swap meets, before making a purchase.

Pet Stores

Pet stores offer a number of benefits to keepers shopping for tegus, including convenience: They usually stock all of the equipment your new lizard needs, including cages, heating devices and food items.

Additionally, they offer you the chance to inspect the lizard up close before purchase. In some cases, you may be able to choose from more than one specimen. Many pet stores provide health guarantees for a short period, which provide some recourse if your new pet turns out to be ill.

However, pet stores are not always the ideal place to purchase your new pet. Pet stores are retail establishments, and as such, you will usually pay more for your new pet than you would from a breeder.

Additionally, pet stores rarely know the pedigree of the animals they sell, and they will rarely know the lizard's date of birth, or other pertinent information.

Other drawbacks associated with pet stores primarily relate to the staff's inexperience. While some pet stores concentrate on reptiles and may educate their staff about proper tegu care, many others provide incorrect advice to their customers.

It is also worth considering the increased exposure to pathogens that pet store animals endure, given the constant flow of animals through such facilities.

Reptile Expos
Reptile expos offer another option for purchasing tegus. Reptile expos often feature resellers, breeders and retailers in the same room, all selling various types of tegus and other reptiles.

Often, the prices at such events are quite reasonable and you are often able to select from many different lizards. However, if you have a problem, it may be difficult to find the seller after the event is over.

Breeders
Because they usually offer unparalleled information and support to their customers, breeders are generally the best place for most novices to shop for tegus. Additionally, breeders often know the species well, and are better able to help you learn the husbandry techniques necessary for success. For those seeking one of the rarer tegu species, breeders are often the only option.

The primary disadvantage of buying from a breeder is that you must often make such purchases from a distance, either by phone or via the internet. Nevertheless, most established breeders are happy to provide you with photographs of the animal you will be purchasing, as well as his or her parents.

Selecting Your Tegu

Not all tegus are created equally, so it is important to select a healthy individual that will give you the best chance of success.

Practically speaking, the most important criterion to consider is the health of the animal. However, the sex, age and history of the lizard are also important things to consider.

Health Checklist

Always check your tegu thoroughly for signs of injury or illness before purchasing it. If you are purchasing the animal from someone in a different part of the country, you must inspect it immediately upon delivery. Notify the seller promptly if the animal exhibits any health problems.

Avoid the temptation to acquire or accept a sick or injured animal in hopes of nursing him back to health. Not only are you likely to incur substantial veterinary costs while treating your new pet, you will likely fail in your attempts to restore the lizard to full health. Sick lizards rarely recover in the hands of novices.

Additionally, by purchasing injured or diseased animals, you incentivize poor husbandry on the part of the retailer. If retailers lose money on sick or injured animals, they will take steps to avoid this eventuality, by acquiring healthier stock in the first place, and providing better care for their charges.

As much as is possible, try to observe the following features:

- **Observe the lizard's skin**. It should be free of lacerations and other damage. Pay special attention to those areas that frequently sustain damage, such as the tip of the lizard's tail, the toes and the tip of the snout. A small cut or abrasion may be relatively easy to treat, but significant abrasions and cuts are likely to become infected and require significant treatment.

- **Gently check the lizard's crevices and creases for mites and ticks**. Mites are about the size of a flake of pepper, and they may be black, brown or red. Mites often move about on the lizard, whereas ticks – if attached and feeding – do not move. Avoid purchasing any animal that has either parasite. Additionally, you should avoid purchasing any other animals from this source, as they are likely to harbor parasites as well.

- **Examine the lizard's eyes, ears and nostrils**. The eyes should not be sunken, and they should be free of discharge. The nostrils should be clear and dry – lizards with runny noses or those who blow bubbles are likely to be suffering from a respiratory infection. However, be aware that lizards often get some water in their nostrils while drinking water. This is no cause for concern.

- **Gently palpate the animal and ensure no lumps or anomalies are apparent**. Lumps in the muscles or abdominal cavity may indicate parasites, abscesses or tumors.

- **Observe the lizard's demeanor**. Healthy lizards are aware of their environment and react to stimuli. When active, the lizard should calmly explore his environment. While you may wish to avoid purchasing an aggressive, defensive or flighty animal, these behaviors do not necessarily indicate a health problem.

- **Check the lizard's vent**. The vent should be clean and free of smeared feces. Smeared feces can indicate parasites or bacterial infections.

- **Check the lizard's appetite**. If possible, ask the retailer to feed the lizard a cricket, superworm or roach. A healthy tegu should usually exhibit a strong food drive, although failing to eat is not *necessarily* a bad sign – the lizard may not be hungry.

The Age
Hatchling tegus are very fragile until they reach about one month of age. Before this, they are unlikely to thrive in the hands of beginning keepers.

Accordingly, most beginners should purchase two- or three-month-old juveniles, who have already become well established. Animals of this age tolerate the changes associated with a new home better than very young specimens do. Further, given their larger size, they will better tolerate temperature and humidity extremes than smaller animals will.

The Sex
Unless you are attempting to breed tegus, you should select a male pet, as females are more likely to suffer from reproduction-related health problems than males are.

Most females will produce and deposit egg clutches upon reaching maturity, whether they are housed with a male or not. While this is not necessarily problematic, novices can easily avoid this unnecessary complication by selecting males as pets.

Additionally, males often reach larger sizes than females do, which many keepers find appealing.

Quarantine
Because new animals may have illnesses or parasites that could infect the rest of your collection, it is wise to quarantine all new acquisitions. This means that you should keep any new animal as separated from the rest of your pets as possible. Only once you have ensured that the new animal is healthy should you introduce it to the rest of your collection.

During the quarantine period, you should keep the new lizard in a simplified habitat, with a paper substrate, water bowl, basking spot and a few hiding places. Keep the temperature and humidity at ideal levels.

It is wise to obtain fecal samples from your lizard during the quarantine period. You can take these samples to your veterinarian, who can check them for signs of internal parasites. Always treat any existing parasite infestations before removing the animal from quarantine.

Always tend to quarantined animals last, as this reduces the chances of transmitting pathogens to your healthy animals. Do not wash quarantined water bowls or cage furniture with those belonging to your healthy animals. Whenever possible, use completely separate tools for quarantined animals and those that have been in your collection for some time.

Always be sure to wash your hands thoroughly after handling quarantined animals, their cages or their tools. Particularly careful keepers wear a smock or alternative clothing when handling quarantined animals.

Quarantine new acquisitions for a minimum of 30 days; 60 or 90 days is even better. Many zoos and professional breeders maintain 180- or 360-day-long quarantine periods.

Chapter 6: Providing the Captive Habitat

In most respects, providing tegus with a suitable captive habitat entails functionally replicating the various aspects of their wild habitats.

In addition to providing your pet with an enclosure, you must provide the animal with the correct thermal environment, appropriate humidity, substrate, and suitable cage furniture.

Enclosure

Providing your tegu with appropriate housing is an essential aspect of captive care. In essence, the habitat you provide to your pet becomes his world.

In "the old days," those inclined to keep reptiles had few choices with regard to caging. The two primary options were to build a custom cage from scratch or construct a lid to use with a fish aquarium.

By contrast, modern hobbyists have a variety of options from which to choose. In addition to building custom cages or adapting aquaria, dozens of different cage styles are available – each with different pros and cons.

Remember: There are few absolutes regarding reptile husbandry, and what works for most keepers and lizards may not work for you and your pet. Additionally, advanced keepers are often able to sidestep problems that trouble beginners.

Dimensions

Tegus require a relatively significant amount of space to thrive. Mature, full-grown tegus should have an enclosure with at least 16 square feet (1.5 square meters) of floor space. Hatchlings and juveniles obviously require less space than adults do.

Most tegus appreciate a significant amount of vertical space in their cage. So, you'll want to provide your lizard with a habitat that is at least 2 feet (60 centimeters) tall, and preferably taller.

Aquariums

Aquariums are popular choices for many pet reptiles and they are available at virtually every pet store in the country. However, they have a number of flaws that make them poor choices.

Aquariums are heavy, fragile and built in proportions that favor the behaviors of fish, rather than reptiles. The glass walls of an aquarium are difficult to clean, and can make your lizard feel like he is exposed.

Additionally, aquariums are only accessible through the top of the enclosure, which is problematic for a number of reasons. You'll have to move the cage lights before removing the top, which further complicates matters.

Commercial Cages

Commercially produced reptile enclosures are one of the best options for tegu maintenance. They feature front-opening doors and they are usually made from lightweight, yet rugged plastic.

Many commercial cages feature internal light fixtures, but these serve as a double-edged sword: On the one hand, they may provide a convenient way to provide light or heat to the enclosure, but these lights can serve as a safety hazard for your pets. Additionally, your lizard may hide in the cracks and crevices surrounding the fixtures.

Commercial cages are generally the most expensive option for tegus, but their benefits strongly outweigh this additional expense.

Plastic Storage Containers

Plastic storage containers, such as those used for shoes, sweaters or food, are popular enclosure options for many reptiles, and large models work well for maintaining young tegus.

You'll need to make modifications to most plastic storage boxes to make them suitable for lizard maintenance, but they rarely present significant challenges.

For example, you'll need to add a series of small holes or cut out a "window" over which you can attach fine mesh screen.

Homemade Cages

For keepers with access to tools and the desire and skill to use them, it is possible to construct a homemade cage for your pet.

A number of materials are suitable for cage construction, and each has different pros and cons. Wood is commonly used, but must be adequately sealed to avoid rotting, warping or absorbing offensive odors.

Plastic sheeting is a very good material, but few have the necessary skills, knowledge and tools necessary for cage construction. Additionally, some plastics may have extended off-gassing times.

Glass can be used, whether glued to itself or when used with a frame. Custom-built glass cages can be better than aquariums, as you can design them in dimensions that are appropriate for tegus. Additionally, they can be constructed in such a way that the door is on the front of the cage, rather than the top.

Security and safety are of paramount importance when constructing a custom cage.

Chapter 7: Establishing the Thermal Environment

Providing the proper thermal environment is one of the most important aspects of reptile husbandry. As ectothermic ("cold blooded") animals, tegus rely on the surrounding temperatures to regulate the rate at which their metabolism operates.

Providing a proper thermal environment can mean the difference between a healthy, thriving lizard and one who spends a great deal of time at the veterinarian's office, battling infections and illness.

While individuals may demonstrate slightly different preferences, and different species have slightly different preferences, most active tegus prefer ambient temperatures in the low- to mid-80s Fahrenheit (about 26 to 30 degrees Celsius). Inactive (sleeping) tegus prefer temperatures in the low 70s Fahrenheit (21 to 23 degrees Celsius).

While these are appropriate air temperatures for tegus, they will also require a basking spot during the day, with a temperature of about 90 to 100 degrees Fahrenheit (32 to 37 degrees Celsius).

Providing your lizard with a suitable thermal environment requires the correct approach, the correct heating equipment and the tools necessary for monitoring the thermal environment.

Size-Related Heating Concerns

Before examining the best way to establish a proper thermal environment, it is important to understand that your lizard's body size influences the way in which he heats up and cools off.

Because volume increases more quickly than surface area does with increasing body size, small individuals experience more rapid temperature fluctuations than larger individuals do.

Accordingly, it is imperative to protect small individuals from temperature extremes. Conversely, larger tegus are more tolerant of temperature extremes than smaller individuals are (though they should still be protected from temperature extremes).

Thermal Gradients

In the wild, tegus move between different microhabitats so that they can maintain ideal body temperature as much as possible. You want to provide similar opportunities for your captive lizard by creating a thermal gradient.

The best way to do this is by clustering the heating devices at one end of the habitat, thereby creating a basking spot (the warmest spot in the enclosure).

The temperatures will slowly drop with increasing distance from the basking spot, which creates a *gradient* of temperatures. Barriers, such as branches and vegetation, also help to create shaded patches, which provide additional thermal options.

This mimics the way temperatures vary from one small place to the next in your pet's natural habitat. For example, a wild tegu may burrow under the leaf litter to escape the sun, or move onto a sun-bathed rock to warm up on a cool morning.

By establishing a gradient in the enclosure, your captive lizard will be able to access a range of different temperatures, which will allow him to manage his body temperature just as his wild counterparts do.

Adjust the heating device until the surface temperatures at the basking spot are between 90 and 100 degrees Fahrenheit (32 to 37 degrees Celsius). Provide a slightly cooler basking spot for immature individuals, with maximum temperatures of about 92 degrees Fahrenheit (33 degrees Celsius).

Because there is no heat source at the other end of the cage, the ambient temperature will gradually fall as your lizard moves away from the heat source. Ideally, the cool end of the cage should be in the low 70s Fahrenheit (22 degrees Celsius).

The need to establish a thermal gradient is one of the most compelling reasons to use a roomy cage. In general, the larger the cage, the easier it is to establish a suitable thermal gradient.

Heating Equipment

There are a variety of different heating devices you can use to keep your tegu's habitat within the appropriate temperature range.

Be sure to consider your choice carefully, and select the best type of heating device for you and your lizard.

Heat Lamps

Heat lamps are usually the best choice for supplying heat to your tegu's habitat. Heat lamps consist of a reflector dome and an incandescent bulb. The light bulb produces heat (in addition to light) and the metal reflector dome directs the heat to a spot inside the cage.

You will need to clamp the lamp to a stable anchor or part of the cage's frame. Always be sure that the lamp is securely attached and will not be dislodged by vibration, children or pets.

Because fire safety is always a concern, and many keepers use high-wattage lightbulbs, opt for heavy-duty reflector domes with ceramic bases, rather than economy units with plastic bases. The price difference is negligible, given the stakes.

One of the greatest benefits of using heat lamps to maintain the temperature of your pet's habitat is the flexibility they offer. While you can adjust the amount of heat provided by heat tapes and other devices with a rheostat or thermostat, you can adjust the enclosure temperature provided by heat lamps in two ways:

- Changing the Bulb Wattage

The simplest way to adjust the temperature of your tegu's cage is by changing the wattage of the bulb you are using.

For example, if a 40-watt light bulb is not raising the temperature of the basking spot high enough, you may try a 60-watt bulb. Alternatively, if a 100-watt light bulb is elevating the cage temperatures higher than are appropriate, switching to a 60-watt bulb may help.

- Adjusting the Distance between the Heat Lamp and the Basking Spot

The closer the heat lamp is to the cage, the warmer the cage will be. If the habitat is too warm, you can move the light farther from the enclosure, which should lower the basking spot temperatures slightly.

However, the farther away you move the lamp, the larger the basking spot becomes. It is important to be careful that you do not move it to far away, which will reduce the effectiveness of the thermal gradient by heating the enclosure too uniformly. In very large cages, this may not compromise the thermal gradient very much, but in a small cage, it may eliminate the "cool side" of the habitat.

In other words, if your heat lamp creates a basking spot that is roughly 1-foot in diameter when it is 1 inch away from the screen, it will produce a slightly cooler, but larger basking spot when moved back another 6 inches or so.

Ceramic Heat Emitters

Ceramic heat emitters are small inserts that function similarly to light bulbs, except that they do not produce any visible light – they only produce heat.

Ceramic heat emitters are used in reflector-dome fixtures, just as heat lamps are. The benefits of such devices are numerous:

- They typically last much longer than light bulbs do

- They are suitable for use with thermostats

- They allow for the creation of overhead basking spots, as lights do

- They can be used day or night

However, the devices do have three primary drawbacks:

- They are very hot when in operation

- They are much more expensive than light bulbs

- You cannot tell by looking if they are hot or cool. This can be a safety hazard – touching a ceramic heat emitter while it is hot is likely to cause serious burns.

Radiant Heat Panels

Quality radiant heat panels are a great choice for heating most reptile habitats, including those containing tegus. Radiant heat panels are essentially heat pads that stick to the roof of the habitat.

They usually feature rugged, plastic or metal casings and internal reflectors to direct the infrared heat back into the cage.

Radiant heat panels have a number of benefits over traditional heat lamps and under tank heat pads:

- They do not produce visible light, which means they are useful for both diurnal and nocturnal heat production. They can be used in conjunction with fluorescent light fixtures during the day, and remain on at night once the lights go off.

- They are inherently flexible. Unlike many devices that do not work well with pulse-proportional thermostats, most radiant heat panels work well with on-off and pulse-proportional thermostats.

The only real drawback to radiant heat panels is their cost: radiant heat panels often cost about two to three times the price of light- or heat pad-oriented systems. However, many radiant heat panels outlast light bulbs and heat pads, a fact that offsets their high initial cost over the long term.

A black and gold tegu.

Heat Pads

Heat pads are an attractive option for many new keepers, but they are not without drawbacks.

- Heat pads have a high risk for causing contact burns.

- If they malfunction, they can damage the cage as well as the surface on which they are placed.

- They are more likely to cause a fire than heat lamps or radiant heat panels are.

However, if installed properly (which includes allowing fresh air to flow over the exposed side of the heat pad) and used in conjunction with a thermostat, they can be reasonably safe. With heat pads, it behooves the keeper to purchase premium products, despite the small increase in price.

Heat Tape
Heat tape is somewhat akin to a "stripped down" heat pad. In fact, most heat pads are simply pieces of heat tape that have already been connected and sealed inside a plastic envelope.

Heat tape is primarily used to heat large numbers of cages simultaneously. It is generally inappropriate for novices, and requires the keeper to make electrical connections. Additionally, a thermostat is always required when using heat tape.

Historically, heat tape was used to keep water pipes from freezing – not to heat reptile cages. While some commercial heat tapes have been designed specifically for reptiles, many have not. Accordingly, it may be illegal, not to mention dangerous, to use heat tapes for purposes other than for which they are designed.

Heat Cables
Heat cables are similar to heat tape, in that they heat a long strip of the cage, but they are much more flexible and easy to use. Many heat cables are suitable to use inside the cage, while others are designed for use outside the habitat.

Always be sure to purchase heat cables that are designed to be used in reptile cages. Those sold at hardware stores are not appropriate for use in a cage.

Heat cables must be used in conjunction with a thermostat, or, at the very least, a rheostat.

Hot Rocks

In the early days of commercial reptile products, faux rocks, branches and caves with internal heating elements were very popular. However, they have generally fallen out of favor among modern keepers. These rocks and branches were often made with poor craftsmanship and cheap materials, causing them to fail and produce tragic results. Additionally, many keepers used the rocks improperly, leading to injuries, illnesses and death for many unfortunate reptiles.

Heated rocks are not designed to heat an entire cage; they are designed to provide a localized source of heat for the reptile. Nevertheless, many keepers tried to use them as the primary heat source for the cage, resulting in dangerously cool cage temperatures.

When lizards must rely on small, localized heat sources placed in otherwise chilly cages, they often hug these heat sources for extended periods of time. This can lead to serious thermal burns – whether or not the unit functions properly. This illustrates the key reason why these devices make adequate supplemental heat sources, but they should not be used as primary heating sources.

Modern heated rocks utilize better features, materials and craftsmanship than the old models did, but they still offer few benefits to the keeper or the kept. Additionally, any heating devices that are designed to be used inside the cage necessitate passing an electric cable through a hole, which is not always easy to accomplish. However, some cages do feature passageways for chords.

Nocturnal Temperatures

Because tegus safely tolerate temperatures in the low-70s Fahrenheit (21 to 22 degrees Celsius) at night, most keepers can allow their pet's habitat to fall to ambient room temperature at night.

Because it is important to avoid using lights on your tegu's habitat at night, those living in homes with lower nighttime temperatures will need to employ additional heat sources. Most such keepers accomplish this through the use of ceramic heat emitters.

Thermometers

It is important to monitor the cage temperatures very carefully to ensure your pet stays health. Just as a water test kit is an aquarist's best friend, quality thermometers are some of the most important husbandry tools for reptile keepers.

Ambient and Surface Temperatures

Two different types of temperature are relevant for pet lizards: ambient temperatures and surface temperatures.

The ambient temperature in your animal's enclosure is the air temperature; the surface temperatures are the temperatures of the objects in the cage. Both are important to monitor, as they can differ widely.

Measure the cage's ambient temperatures with a digital thermometer. An indoor-outdoor model will feature a probe that allows you to measure the temperature at both ends of the thermal gradient at once. For example, you may position the thermometer at the cool side of the cage, but attach the remote probe to a branch near the basking spot.

Because standard digital thermometers do not measure surface temperatures well, use a non-contact, infrared thermometer for such measurements. These devices will allow you to measure surface temperatures accurately from a short distance away.

Thermostats and Rheostats

Some heating devices, such as heat lamps, are designed to operate at full capacity for the entire time that they are turned on. Such devices should not be used with thermostats – instead, care should be taken to calibrate the proper temperature by tweaking the bulb wattage.

Other devices, such as heat pads, heat tape and radiant heat panels are designed to be used with a regulating device, such as a thermostat or rheostat, which maintains the proper temperature

Rheostats

Rheostats are similar to light-dimmer switches, and they allow you to reduce the output of a heating device. In this way, you can dial in the proper temperature for the habitat.

The drawback to rheostats is that they only regulate the amount of power going to the device – they do not monitor the cage temperature or adjust the power flow automatically. In practice, even with the same level of power entering the device, the amount of heat generated by most heat sources will vary over the course of the day.

If you set the rheostat so that it keeps the cage at the right temperature in the morning, it may become too hot by the middle of the day. Conversely, setting the proper temperature during the middle of the day may leave the morning temperatures too cool.

Care must be taken to ensure that the rheostat controller is not inadvertently bumped or jostled, causing the temperature to rise or fall outside of healthy parameters.

Thermostats

Thermostats are similar to rheostats, except that they also feature a temperature probe that monitors the temperature in the cage (or under the basking source). This allows the thermostat to adjust the power going to the device as necessary to maintain a predetermined temperature.

For example, if you place the temperature probe under a basking spot powered by a radiant heat panel, the thermostat will keep the temperature relatively constant under the basking site.

There are two different types of thermostats:

- On-Off Thermostats

On-Off Thermostats work by cutting the power to the device when the probe's temperature reaches a given temperature. For example, if the thermostat were set to 85 degrees Fahrenheit (29 degrees Celsius), the heating device would turn off whenever the temperature exceeds this threshold. When the temperature falls below 85, the thermostat restores power to the unit, and the heater begins functioning again. This cycle will continue to repeat, thus maintaining the temperature within a relatively small range.

Be aware that on-off thermostats have a "lag" factor, meaning that they do not turn off when the temperature reaches a given temperature. They turn off when the temperature is a few degrees above that temperature, and then turn back on when the temperate is a little below the set point. Because of this, it is important to avoid setting the temperature at the limits of your pet's acceptable range. Some premium models have an adjustable amount of threshold for this factor, which is helpful.

- Pulse Proportional Thermostats

Pulse proportional thermostats work by constantly sending pulses of electricity to the heater. By varying the rate of pulses, the amount of energy reaching the heating devices varies. A small computer inside the thermostat adjusts this rate to match the set-point temperature as measured by the probe. Accordingly, pulse proportional thermostats maintain much more consistent temperatures than on-off thermostats do.

Lights should not be used with thermostats, as the constant flickering may stress your pet. Conversely, heat pads, heat tape, radiant heat panels and ceramic heat emitters should always be used with either a rheostat or, preferably, a thermostat to avoid overheating your tegu.

Thermostat Failure

If used for long enough, all thermostats eventually fail. The question is will yours fail today or twenty years from now. While some thermostats fail in the "off" position, a thermostat that fails in the "on" position may overheat your lizards. Unfortunately, tales of entire collections being lost to a faulty thermostat are too common.

Accordingly, it behooves the keeper to acquire high-quality thermostats. Some keepers use two thermostats, connected in series arrangement. By setting the second thermostat (the "backup thermostat") a few degrees higher than the setting used on the "primary thermostat," you safeguard yourself against the failure of either unit.

In such a scenario, the backup thermostat allows the full power coming to it to travel through to the heating device, as the temperature never reaches its higher set-point temperature.

However, if the first unit fails in the "on" position, the second thermostat will keep the temperatures from rising too high. The temperature will rise a few degrees in accordance with the higher set-point temperature, but it will not get hot enough to harm your pets.

If the backup thermostat fails in the "on" position, the first thermostat retains control. If either fails in the "off" position, the temperature will fall until you rectify the situation, but a brief exposure to relatively cool temperatures is unlikely to be fatal.

Chapter 8: Lighting the Enclosure

Sunlight plays an important role in the lives of most diurnal lizards, including tegus.

It is always preferable to provide your tegu with access to unfiltered sunlight, but this is not always possible. In these cases, it is necessary to provide your lizard with high quality lighting, which can partially replace the light created by the sun.

Tegus deprived of appropriate lighting may become seriously ill. Learning how to provide the proper lighting for reptiles is sometimes an arduous task for beginners, but it is very important to the long-term health of your pet that you do. To understand the type of light your lizard needs, you must first understand a little bit about light.

The Electromagnetic Spectrum

Light is a type of energy that physicists call electromagnetic radiation; it travels in waves. These waves may differ in amplitude, which correlates to the vertical distance between consecutive wave crests and troughs, frequency, which correlates with the number of crests per unit of time, and wavelength.

Wavelength is the distance from one crest to the next, or one trough to the next. Wavelength and frequency are inversely proportional, meaning that as the wavelength increases, the frequency decreases. It is more common for reptile keepers to discuss wavelengths rather than frequencies.

The sun produces energy (light) with a very wide range of constituent wavelengths. Some of these wavelengths fall within a range called the visible spectrum; humans can detect these rays with their eyes. Such waves have wavelengths between about 390 and 700 nanometers. Rays with wavelengths longer or shorter than these limits are broken into their own groups and given different names.

Those rays with around 390 nanometer wavelengths or less are called ultraviolet rays or UV rays. UV rays are broken down into three different categories, just as the different colors correspond with different wavelengths of visible light. UVA rays have wavelengths between 315 to 400 nanometers, while UVB rays have wavelengths between 280 and 315 nanometers while UVC rays have wavelengths between 100 and 280 nanometers.

Rays with wavelengths of less than 280 nanometers are called x-rays and gamma rays. At the other end of the spectrum, infrared rays have wavelengths longer than 700 nanometers; microwaves and radio waves are even longer.

UVA rays are important for food recognition, appetite, activity and eliciting natural behaviors. UVB rays are necessary for many reptiles to produce vitamin D3. Without this vitamin, reptiles cannot properly metabolize their calcium.

Light Color

The light that comes from the sun and light bulbs is composed of a combination of wavelengths, which create the blended white light that you perceive. This combination of wavelengths varies slightly from one light source to the next.

The sun produces very balanced white light, while "economy" incandescent bulbs produce relatively fewer blue rays and yields a yellow-looking light. High-quality bulbs designed for reptiles often produce very balanced, white light. The degree to which light causes objects to look as they would under sunlight is called the Color Rendering Index, or CRI. Sunlight has a CRI of 100, while quality bulbs have CRIs of 80 to 90; by contrast, a typical incandescent bulb has a CRI of 40 to 50

Light Brightness

Another important characteristic of light that relates to lizards is luminosity, or the brightness of light. Measured in units called Lux, luminosity is an important consideration for your lighting system. While you cannot possibly replicate the intensity of the sun's light, it is desirable in most circumstances to ensure the habitat is lit as well as is reasonably possible.

Without access to appropriately bright lighting, many reptiles become lethargic, depressed or exhibit hibernating behaviors. Dim lighting may inhibit feeding and cause lizards to become stressed and ill.

However, while it is important to provide very bright lighting in portions of the cage, you must also provide the lizards with shade, into which they can retreat if they desire.

Your Lizard's Lighting Needs

To reiterate, tegus (and most other diurnal lizards) require:

- Light that is comprised of visible light, as well as UVA and UVB wavelengths

- Light with a high color-rendering index

- Light of the sufficiently strong intensity

Now that you know what your lizard requires, you can go about designing the lighting system for his habitat. Ultraviolet radiation is the most difficult component of proper lighting to provide, so it makes sense to begin by examining the types of bulbs that produce UV radiation.

The only commercially produced bulbs that produce significant amounts of UVA and UVB and suitable for a lizard habitat are linear fluorescent light bulbs, compact fluorescent light bulbs and mercury vapor bulbs.

Neither type of fluorescent bulb produces significant amounts of heat, but mercury vapor bulbs produce a lot of heat and serve a dual function. In many cases, keepers elect to use both types of lights – a mercury vapor bulb for a warm basking site with high levels of UV radiation and fluorescent bulbs to light the rest of the cage without raising the temperature. You can also use fluorescent bulbs to provide the requisite UV radiation and use a regular incandescent bulb to generate the basking spot.

Fluorescent bulbs have a much longer history of use than mercury vapor bulbs, which makes some keepers more comfortable using them. However, many models only produce moderate amounts of UVB radiation. While some mercury vapor bulbs produce significant quantities of UVB, some question the wisdom of producing more UV radiation than the animal receives in the wild.

Additionally, mercury vapor bulbs are much too powerful to use in small habitats, and they are more expensive initially.

Most fluorescent bulbs must be placed within 12 inches of the basking surface, while some mercury vapor bulbs should be placed farther away from the basking surface – be sure to read the manufacturer's instructions before use. Be sure that the bulbs you purchase specifically state the amount of UVB radiation they produce; this figure is expressed as a percentage, for example 7% UVB. Most UVB-producing bulbs require replacement every six to 12 months – whether or not they have stopped producing light.

However, ultraviolet radiation is only one of the characteristics that lizard keepers must consider. The light bulbs used must also produce a sunlight-like spectrum. Fortunately, most high-quality light bulbs that produce significant amounts of UVA and UVB radiation also feature a high color-rendering index. The higher the CRI, the better, but any bulbs with a CRI of 90 or above will work well. If you are having trouble deciding between two otherwise evenly matched bulbs, select the one with the higher CRI value.

Brightness is the final, and easiest, consideration for the keeper to address. While no one yet knows what the ideal luminosity for a tegu's cage is, it makes sense to ensure that part of the cage features very bright lighting. However, you should always offer a shaded retreat within the enclosure into which your lizard can avoid the light if he desires.

Connect the lights to an electric timer to keep the length of the day and night consistent. Most tegus thrive with 12 hours of daylight and 12 hours of darkness all year long. However, it may be helpful to reduce the number of daylight hours during the fall and winter, if you are trying to breed your tegus.

Chapter 9: Substrate and Furniture

Once you have purchased or constructed your tegu's enclosure, you must place appropriate items inside it. In general, these items take the form of an appropriate substrate and the proper cage furniture, which may include live plants, hiding locations and perches for climbing.

Substrate

Substrate is a contentious issue among lizard keepers, and there are a variety of disparate notions about which one works best. We'll examine some of the most popular choices (both good and bad) and recommend that readers make the best choice possible for their lizards.

Bare Enclosure Floors (No Substrate)

If you are using an enclosure with a plastic, glass or laminated floor, you can avoid using any substrate at all. The primary benefit to this approach is that you do not have to worry about your pet inadvertently ingesting some of the substrate during feeding activities.

By skipping the substrate, you can also avoid having to replace it periodically as well as the small associated expense. However, substrate-free maintenance requires more maintenance, as the cage bottom must be cleaned daily.

One drawback to substrate-free husbandry is that water will begin to pool on the cage floor if you mist the cage. This can be messy and accelerate the growth of bacterial colonies. Additionally, your lizard's waste will just sit on the floor until you clean it up. This means you'll need to clean the cage very regularly (once or twice per day) to keep your lizard from being coated in feces or urates.

Substrate-free maintenance is best suited for maintaining hatchlings and juveniles, particularly when they are housed in groups. This approach allows the keeper to reduce the chances that the hatchlings will ingest substrate.

Cypress Mulch

Cypress mulch is a popular substrate choice for tegus. It not only looks attractive and holds humidity well, but cypress mulch typically has a pleasant odor.

One drawback to cypress mulch is that some brands (or individual bags among otherwise good brands) produce a stick-like mulch, rather than mulch composed of thicker pieces. These sharp sticks can injure the keeper and the kept. It usually only takes one cypress mulch splinter jammed under a keeper's fingernail to cause them to switch substrates.

Cypress fibers do represent an ingestion hazard, so keepers using it should always be alert for signs that a captive has consumed anything other than food. Additionally, the numerous nooks and crannies produced by the mulch will provide insects with places to hide.

Cypress mulch is available from most home improvement and garden centers, as well as pet supply retailers. No matter the source you use, be sure that the product contains 100 percent cypress mulch without any demolition or salvage content.

Fir (Orchid) Bark

The bark of fir trees is often used for orchid propagation, and so it is often called "orchid bark." Orchid bark is very attractive, and, thanks to its relatively uniform shape, does not represent as much of an ingestion hazard as cypress mulch does.

Orchid bark absorbs water very well, so it is useful for species that require relatively high humidity levels, such as tegus. Additionally, orchid bark is easy to spot clean. However, monthly replacement can be expensive for those living in the Eastern United States and Europe.

Soils

Soil is another acceptable substrate for tegus. You can make a suitable soil substrate by digging up your own soil, purchasing organic soil products or mixing your own blend.

Avoid products containing perlite, manure, fertilizers, pre-emergent herbicides or other additives. Sterilization of the soil before adding it to the enclosure is not strictly necessary; in fact, many of the microorganisms present will help breakdown waste products from your lizard.

Paper Products

Newspaper, paper towels and commercial cage liners are acceptable for use with tegus, but they offer few benefits over a bare floor. The only real benefit paper substrates offer tegu keepers is that they make it easier to clean the cage floor – you can simply remove the paper each day and replace it with a fresh sheet.

However, paper substrates give insects places to hide, so be sure to check underneath the paper periodically, and flush out any hiding insects.

Substrate Comparison Chart

Substrate	Pros	Cons
No Substrate	No ingestion hazard. Easy to spot clean and sterilize. Free.	Unattractive. Water pools on surface.
Soil	Absorbs and retains water and easy to spot clean.	Ingestion hazard. Messy.
Cypress Mulch	Absorbs and retains water, attractive and easy to spot clean.	Ingestion hazard. Messy. Provides hiding places for insects.
Fir (Orchid) Bark	Absorbs and retains water, attractive and easy to spot clean.	Ingestion hazard. Messy. Expensive.
Newspaper	Absorbs *some* water. Safe, low-cost. Easy to maintain.	Unattractive. Provides hiding places for insects.
Commercial Paper Products	Absorbs *some* water. Safe, low-cost. Easy to maintain and keep clean.	Provides hiding places for insects. Can be expensive.

Substrates to Avoid

Some substrates are completely inappropriate for tegu maintenance, and should be avoided at all costs. These include:

- **Aspen or Pine Shavings** – Wood shavings (as opposed to shredded bark or mulch) are not appropriate substrates for tegus. In addition to representing a choking hazard, wood shavings will quickly rot if they become wet.

- **Cedar Shavings** – Cedar shavings produce toxic fumes that may sicken or kill your tegu. Always avoid cedar shavings.

- **Sand** – Sand is too dusty for tegus. It will also stick to feeder insects and find its way into your lizard's digestive tract.

- **Gravel** – You can use large gravel as a substrate, but its problems outweigh its benefits. Gravel must be washed when soiled, which is laborious and time consuming. Gravel is also quite heavy, which can cause headaches for the keeper.

- **Artificial Turf** – Although it seems like a viable option with a number of benefits, artificial turf is not a good substrate for tegus. Keeping artificial turf clean is difficult, and the threads may come loose and wrap around your lizard's tail, tongue or toes.

Cage Furniture

To complete your tegu's habitat, you must provide him with visual barriers to help keep his stress level low, and perches, which he can use to travel through his cage.

A great way to provide visual barriers for your tegus is to add cork slabs, cardboard tubes or live plants to the enclosure.

All perches must be safe, easy to clean and securely attached to the enclosure. Most keepers opt for real branches, but you can also use commercially produced plastic vines or branches.

Cork bark

The outer bark of the cork oak (*Quercus suber*), cork bark is available in both tubes and flat slabs. Either work well for tegu maintenance, although flat slabs can be arranged to provide your lizard with snugger hiding places.

The primary downsides to cork bark relate to its price (it is often rather expensive) and its tendency to collect debris in the cracks on its surface, which makes cleaning difficult.

Cardboard and Other Disposable Hides

Cardboard tubes, boxes or sheets also make excellent hiding spaces, as do sections of foam egg crate. These materials are light weight, very low cost and easy to replace once soiled.

Try to arrange these items in ways that mimic the hiding places tegus would use in the wild. For example, tegus like to hide in burrows, so you could place a cardboard tube along the back of the enclosure.

Plants

Live plants may require more work and effort on the part of the keeper, but they offer several benefits for your pet. In addition to providing a place for your pet to slip out of sight, live plants increase the humidity of the enclosure.

Always wash all plants before placing them in the enclosure to help remove any pesticide residues. It is also wise to discard the potting soil used for the plant and replace it with fresh soil, which you know contains no pesticides, perlite or fertilizer.

While you can plant cage plants directly in soil substrates, this complicates maintenance and makes it difficult to replace the substrate regularly. Accordingly, it is generally preferable to keep the plant in some type of container. Be sure to use a catch tray under the pot, so that water draining from the container does not flow into the cage.

You must use care to select a species that will thrive in your tegu's enclosure. For example, species that require direct sunlight will perish in the relatively dim light in your pet's home.

Instead, you must choose plants that will thrive in shaded conditions. Similarly, because you will be misting the cage regularly, and trying to keep the internal environment as humid as possible, few succulents or other plants adapted to arid habitats will live in a tegu enclosure.

As much as is possible, choose plants that have broad leaves, which will allow them to serve as visual barriers for your lizard.

Perches

Although climbing branches or perches are not absolutely necessary for tegu maintenance, but they can provide your pet with more useable cage space and allow you to observe natural behaviors.

You can purchase climbing branches from pet and craft stores, or you can collect them yourself. When collecting your own branches, try to use branches that are still attached to trees (always obtain permission first). Such branches will harbor fewer insects and other invertebrate pests than dead branches will.

Many different types of branches can be used in tegu cages. Most non-aromatic hardwoods suffice.

Whenever collecting wood to be used as perches, bring a ruler so that you can visualize how large the branch will be, once it is back in the cage. Leave several inches of spare material at each end of the branch; this way, you can cut the perch to the correct length, once you arrive back home.

Always wash branches with plenty of hot water and a stiff, metal-bristled scrub brush to remove as much dirt, dust and fungus as possible before placing them in your pet's cage. Clean stubborn spots with a little bit of dish soap, but be sure to rinse them thoroughly afterwards.

It is also advisable to sterilize branches before placing them in a cage. The easiest way to do so is by placing the branch in a 350-degree oven for about 15 minutes. Doing so should kill the vast majority of pests and pathogens lurking inside the wood.

Some keepers like to cover their branches with a water-sealing product. This is acceptable if a non-toxic product is used and the branches are allowed to air dry for several days before being placed in the cage. However, as branches are relatively easy to replace, it is not necessary to seal them if you plan to replace them.

When placing the perches in the cage, be sure to do so in a way that allows your pet to access all areas of the cage. Try to strike a good balance between offering your pet plenty of perches, without overly crowding the habitat.

You can often place branches diagonally across the enclosure, in such a way that alleviates the need for direct attachment to the cage. However, horizontal branches will require secure points of attachment so they do not fall and injure your pet.

You can attach the branches to the cage in a variety of different ways. Be sure to make it easy to remove the branches as necessary, so you can clean them or transfer your lizard without having to handle him.

You can use hooks and eye-screws to suspend branches, which allows for quick and easy removal, but it is only applicable for cages with walls that will accept and support the eye-screws. You can also make "closet rod holders" by cutting a slot into small PVC caps, which are attached to the cage frame.

Chapter 10: Maintaining the Captive Habitat

Now that you have acquired your lizard and set up the enclosure, you must develop a protocol for maintaining his habitat. While tegu habitats require major maintenance every month or so, they only require minor daily maintenance. In addition to designing a husbandry protocol, you must embrace a record-keeping system to track your lizard's growth and health.

Cleaning and Maintenance Procedures

Once you have decided on the proper enclosure for your pet, you must keep your lizard fed, hydrated and ensure that the habitat stays in proper working order to keep your captive healthy and comfortable.

Some tasks must be completed each day, while others are should be performed weekly, monthly or annually.

Daily

- Monitor the ambient and surface temperatures of the habitat.

- Provide drinking water by misting the cage.

- Spot clean the cage to remove any loose insects, feces, urates or pieces of shed skin.

- Ensure that the lights, latches and other moving parts are in working order.

- Verify that your lizard is acting normally and appears healthy. You do not necessarily need to handle him to do so.

- Feed your lizard a few insects (some keepers only feed their captives three or four times per week).

- Ensure that the humidity and ventilation are at appropriate levels.

Weekly

- Change sheet-like substrates (newspaper, paper towels, etc.).

- Clean the inside surfaces of the enclosure.

- Inspect your lizard closely for any signs of injury, parasites or illness.

- Wash and sterilize all food dishes.

Monthly
- Break down the cage completely, remove and discard particulate substrates.

- Sterilize drip containers and similar equipment in a mild bleach solution.

- Measure and weigh your lizard.

- Photograph your pet (recommended, but not imperative).

- Prune any plants as necessary.

Annually
- Replace the batteries in your thermometers and any other devices that use them.

- Replace UVB lights (some require replacement every six months)

Cleaning your lizard's cage and furniture is relatively simple. Regardless of the way it became soiled, the basic process remains the same:

1. Rinse the object
2. Using a scrub brush or sponge and soapy water, remove any organic debris from the object.
3. Rinse the object thoroughly.
4. Disinfect the object.
5. Re-rinse the object.
6. Dry the object.

Chemicals & Tools
A variety of chemicals and tools are necessary for reptile care. Save yourself some time by purchasing dedicated cleaning products and keeping them in the same place that you keep your tools.

Spray Bottles
Misting your tegu and his habitat with fresh water is one of the best ways to provide him with an appropriate humidity level. You can do

this with a small, handheld misting bottle or a larger, pressurized unit (such as those used to spray herbicides). Automated units are available, but they are rarely cost-effective unless you are caring for a large colony of tegus.

Scrub Brushes or Sponges
It helps to have a few different types of scrub brushes and sponges on hand for scrubbing and cleaning different items. Use the least abrasive sponge or brush suitable for the task to prevent wearing out cage items prematurely. Do not use abrasive materials on glass or acrylic surfaces. Steel-bristled brushes work well for scrubbing coarse, wooden items, such as branches.

Spatulas and Putty Knives
Spatulas, putty knives and similar tools are often helpful for cleaning reptile cages. For example, urates (which are not soluble in anything short of hot lava) often become stuck on cage walls or furniture. Instead of trying to dissolve them with harsh chemicals, just scrape them away with a sturdy plastic putty knife.

Spatulas and putty knives can also be helpful for removing wet newspaper, which often becomes stuck to the floor of the cage.

Small Vacuums
Small, handheld vacuums are very helpful for sucking up the dust left behind from substrates. They are also helpful for cleaning the cracks and crevices around the cage doors. A shop vacuum, with suitable hoses and attachments, can also be helpful, if you have enough room to store it.

Steam Cleaners
Steam cleaners are very effective for sterilizing cages, water bowls and durable cage props after they have been cleaned. In fact, steam is often a better choice than chemical disinfectants, as it will not leave behind a toxic residue. Never use a steam cleaner near your lizard, the plants in his cage or any other living organisms.

Soap
Use a gentle, non-scented dish soap. Antibacterial soap is preferred, but not necessary. Most people use far more soap than is necessary -- a few drops mixed with a quantity of water is usually sufficient to help remove surface pollutants.

Bleach
Bleach (diluted to one-half cup per gallon of water) makes an excellent disinfectant. Be careful not to spill any on clothing, carpets or furniture, as it is likely to discolor the objects.

Always be sure to rinse objects thoroughly after using bleach and be sure that you cannot detect any residual odor. Bleach does not work as a disinfectant when in contact with organic substances; accordingly, items must be cleaned before you can disinfect them.

Veterinarian Approved Disinfectant
Many commercial products are available that are designed to be safe for their pets. Consult with your veterinarian about the best product for your situation, its method of use and its proper dilution.

Avoid Phenols
Always avoid cleaners that contain phenols, as they are extremely toxic to some reptiles. In general, do not use household cleaning products to avoid exposing your pet to toxic chemicals.

Keeping Records

It is important to keep records regarding your pet's health, growth and feeding, as well as any other important details. In the past, reptile keepers would do so on small index cards or in a notebook. In the modern world, technological solutions may be easier. For example, you can use your computer or mobile device to keep track of the pertinent info about your pet.

You can record as much information about your pet as you like, and the more information to you record, the better. But minimally, you should record the following:

Pedigree and Origin Information
Be sure to record the source of your lizard, the date on which you acquired him and any other data that is available. Breeders will often provide customers with information regarding the sire, dam, date of birth, weights and feeding records, but other sources will rarely offer comparable data.

Feeding Information

Record the date of each feeding, as well as the type of food item(s) offered. It is also helpful to record any preferences you may observe or any meals that are refused.

It is also wise to record the times you supplement the food with calcium or vitamin powders, unless you employ a standard weekly protocol.

Weights and Length

Because you look at your pet frequently, it is difficult to appreciate how quickly he is (or isn't) growing. Accordingly, it is important to track his size diligently.

Weigh your tegu with a high quality digital scale. The scale must be sensitive to one-tenth-gram increments to be useful for very small lizards.

It is often easiest to use a dedicated "weighing container" with a known weight to measure your tegu. This way, you will not have to keep the lizard stationary on the scale's platform – you can simply place him in the container and place the entire container on the scale. Subtract the weight of the container to obtain the weight of your lizard.

You can measure your lizard's length as well, but it is not as important as tracking his weight. Be sure to measure his snout-vent length, rather than his total length, in case he eventually loses a portion of his tail. One easy way to get an approximation of your tegu's length is to place him in a clear-bottomed container, alongside a ruler. Lift the container above your head and look through the bottom of the container to compare your lizard's length against the ruler.

Maintenance Information

Record all of the noteworthy events associated with your pet's care. While it is not necessary to note that you misted the cage each day, it is appropriate to record the dates on which you changed the substrate or sterilized the cage.

Whenever you purchase new equipment, supplies or caging, note the date and source. This not only helps to remind you when you purchased the items, but it may help you track down a source for the items in the future, if necessary.

Breeding Information

If you intend to breed your lizard, you should record all details associated with pre-breeding conditioning, cycling, introductions, matings, color changes, copulations and egg deposition. Record all pertinent information about any resulting clutches as well, including the number of viable eggs, as well as the number of unhatched and unfertilized eggs (often called "slugs" by reptile keepers). Additionally, if you keep several lizards together in the same enclosure, you'll want to be careful to document the details of egg deposition, so you can be sure you know the correct parentage of each egg.

Record Keeping Samples

The following are two different examples of suitable recording systems. The first example is reminiscent of the style employed by many with large collections. Because such keepers often have numerous animals, the notes are very simple, and require a minimum amount of writing or typing.

The second example demonstrates a simple approach that is employed by many with small collections (or a single pet): keeping notes on paper. Such notes could be taken in a notebook or journal, or you could type directly into a word processor. It does not matter *how* you keep records, just that you *do* keep records.

ID Number:	44522	Genus: Species/Sub:	Tupinambis teguixin	Gender: DOB:	Male 3/20/14	CARD #2
6.30.15 Crickets	7.03.15 Super Worms	7.08.15 Fruit mix	7.14.15 Crickets	7.17.15 Roaches		
7.01.15 Crickets	7.05.15 Small mouse	7.09.15 Roaches	7.15.15 Fruit Mix	7.19.15 Sterilized Cage		

7.02.15	7.06.15	7.12.15	7.16.15			
Fruit mix	Crickets	Small mouse	Crickets			

Date	Notes
4-22-13	*Acquired "Terry the Tegu" from a lizard breeder named Mark at the in-town reptile expo. Mark explained that Tommy's scientific name is Tupinambis teguixin. Cost was $85. Mark said he purchased the lizard in March, but he does not know the exact date.*
4-23-13	*Terry spent the night in the container I bought him in. I purchased a small plastic storage box cage, a heat lamp and a thermometer at the hardware store, and I ordered a non-contact thermometer online. I found and cleaned a few branches from outside, and a pothos plant so he had places to climb and hide*
4-27-13	*Terry eagerly drank when I put a water dish in front of him. He was also hungry! He ate 12 crickets in about 5 minutes.*
4-29-13	*I fed Terry 18 crickets today. He ate them as quickly as the first feeding*
5-1-13	*Since Terry looked hungry, I fed him a roach today. I caught it outside, but I'll start buying some too.*
5-3-13	*Fed Terry a dozen crickets and a bit of fruit mix I made.*

Chapter 11: Feeding Tegus

Feeding your tegu a healthy diet is one of the most important aspects of his care. This not only means providing your pet with suitable food items, but providing them in the proper way, in the appropriate amounts and on a proper schedule.

Types of Food

Tegus are omnivores that consume a wide variety of foods in the wild. Some of the food categories that should be included in your lizard's captive diet are detailed below.

Insects

Insects should form an important part of your tegu's diet – especially while he is still young. Crickets or roaches make a nice staple, while the other insects can be incorporated to add variety.

Most experienced keepers avoid feeding wild caught insects to their tegus, as the insects may be contaminated with pesticides or infested with parasites.

The following insects make suitable prey for tegus:

- Crickets

- Roaches

- Mealworms

- Giant Mealworms

- Superworms

- Wax Worms

- Grasshoppers

Rodents

Rodents are also a good food item for tegus large enough to consume them. However, care must be taken to avoid causing your lizard to become obese, given the high caloric value of mice and rats.

Rodents are available commercially in a range of sizes, from hairless, newborn "pinkies,' to fully-grown, retired breeders. Whenever possible, stick to rodents who have already developed body hair, as these will have better-developed skeletal systems, which will provide more of the calcium your lizard needs to survive.

Birds

Chicks, quail and ducks are often available commercially, and they make excellent food sources for larger tegus. Some keepers avoid providing birds to their pet, as they often cause tegus to produce soft, foul-smelling feces. Additionally, feeding a bird-based diet likely increases the chances that your lizard will contract salmonella.

Nevertheless, chicks and other birds can serve as a viable food source for tegus.

Eggs

Eggs are an excellent occasional supplementary food item for your lizards. Boil them until the yolk sets, which will reduce the bacterial load present in the egg. Eggs make up a significant portion of the diet of some species, and it is one of the few "human" foods that are suitable for tegus. Your tegu may eat the whole egg if he is big enough, or he may break it and lap out the contents.

Smaller lizards can be offered full sized eggs, but you can also find quail eggs at some grocery stores.

Plant Material

Tegus consume quite a bit of plant material in the wild, and keepers are wise to provide plenty of fresh fruits and vegetables to their captives.

Some of the best fruits and vegetables to offer your lizard include:

- Mango

- Apple

- Pear

- Blueberries

- Blackberries

- Raspberries

- Grapes

- Melon

- Pumpkin

- Kiwi

- Strawberries

- Squash

- Zucchini

- Collard greens

- Mustard greens

- Turnip greens

- Bok choy

- Romaine lettuce

- Broccoli

- Carrots

- Corn

- Cauliflower

- Beans

- Peas

Be sure to rinse all fruits before offering them to your lizard to remove any pesticide residues or dirt. Additionally, grate or cut all fruits and vegetables into small pieces, which your lizard can easily ingest.

Live, Fresh Killed or Frozen

Tegus are completely capable of dispatching suitably sized prey, but it is best to offer frozen-thawed or pre-killed rodents and birds to your pet. Not only is it possible that a rodent or bird may injure your lizard, being stalked, captured and eaten by a hungry lizard is very stressful (to say the least) for the mouse, rat or bird. It is preferable to euthanize prey animals humanely or purchase those that are frozen.

Freezing also kills some pathogens, so frozen-thawed rodents are likely healthier for your tegu.

Prey Size

Tegus can eat large meals, but there is no need to provide food at the upper end of their comfort range. In general, food items should be smaller than the space between the lizard's eyes.

This is especially important for young animals, whose heads are very large relative to their body size. Tegus can experience problems from swallowing prey that is too big, and it often causes them to vomit.

How to Offer Food

You can simply release crickets and other insects into your tegu's cage. This will also provide exercise and mental stimulation for your pet. However, it is often better to place burrowing insects – mealworms, roaches, etc. – on a feeding dish so that they do not tunnel out of sight.

Some keepers like to place a group of mealworms on a plate, and then cover them with a big pile of dirt or mulch. The lizard will usually smell the insects, and get exercise by digging them out of the dirt or mulch.

Do not allow large numbers of feeder insects to roam the enclosure freely, as it can stress your pet. Additionally, the crickets may feed on your lizard's delicate skin near his eyes and vent.

This does not mean that you cannot offer a large lizard a significant number of insects at one time. It just means that you should only give your tegu as many insects as he can eat in a short period of time. Once he is full, the cage should be free of insects.

Offer your tegu frozen rodents or birds by dangling these items in front of their face with long tongs or tweezers. Tegus get very excited at feeding time, so you must be careful to avoid their sharp teeth.

Fruits and vegetables should be offered on a plate, dish or flat, clean rock.

Feeding Frequency

The proper feeding frequency for your tegu depends on his size, species and age. Generally speaking, tegus should be fed three to six times per week; the younger the lizard, the more often it should be fed.

As long as your tegu is healthy, gets plenty of exercise, has access to suitable temperatures and is provided with a wide variety of food items, you do not have to worry about over-feeding him. However, mature animals – or those living in small cages – may become overweight if fed too frequently.

Ultimately, you must adjust your lizard's diet by monitoring his weight regularly. Young lizards should exhibit steady, moderate growth rates, while mature animals should maintain a relatively consistent body weight.

If your lizard begins losing weight, you must increase the frequency of his feedings. Conversely, those that gain excessive wait should be placed on restrictive diets. Consult with your veterinarian before altering your feeding schedule drastically.

Vitamin and Mineral Supplements

Many keepers add commercially produced vitamin and mineral supplements to their tegu's food on a regular basis. In theory, these supplements help to correct dietary deficiencies and ensure that captive lizards get a balanced diet. In practice, things are not this simple.

While some vitamins and minerals are unlikely to build up to toxic levels, others may very well cause problems if provided in excess. This means that you cannot simply apply supplements to every meal – you must decide upon a sensible supplementation schedule.

Additionally, it can be difficult to ascertain exactly how much of the various vitamins and minerals you will be providing to your lizard, as most such products are sold as fine powders, designed to be sprinkled on feeder insects.

This is hardly a precise way to provide the proper dose to your lizard, and the potential for grossly over- or under-estimating the amount of supplement delivered is very real.

Because the age, sex and health of your tegu all influence the amount of vitamins and minerals your pet requires, and each individual product has a unique composition, it is wise to consult your veterinarian before deciding upon a supplementation schedule.

However, most keepers provide vitamin supplementation once each week, and calcium supplementation several times per week.

Chapter 12: Providing Water to Your Tegu

Like most other animals, tegus require drinking water to remain healthy. However, the relative humidity (the amount of water in the air) is also an important factor in their health.

While drinking water helps to keep the lizards hydrated, the moisture in the air helps to keep their skin healthy and prevents respiratory problems from developing.

Providing Drinking Water

Providing ample drinking water is imperative to the health of your tegu. Most tegus will drink from a water dish, which makes it easy to keep them properly hydrated.

Make sure your tegu has water available at all times, and be sure to wash the water bowl out with soap and water every day. Water dishes can become contaminated with bacteria very easily, which can make your lizard ill.

Water Quality

Some keepers prefer to give their lizard dechlorinated or purified or spring water, but others simply offer tap water. Purified bottled water and spring water are typically safe for lizards, but distilled water should be avoided to prevent causing electrolyte imbalances.

It is wise to have tap water tested to ensure that heavy metals or other pollutants are not present before offering it to your pet.

Humidity

Most tegus hail from moderately humid habitats (although many live in areas with regular dry seasons), and it is wise to provide them with such in captive settings.

In addition to helping them shed their skin more effectively, appropriate humidity is also important for the health of their respiratory system.

Reptile keepers usually achieve such humidity levels by restricting the airflow into the cage, adding more water to the enclosure or some combination of both strategies.

Most keepers add water to the cage by misting the cage and plants inside the enclosure with lukewarm water on a daily basis. The resulting water droplets will help to raise the cage's humidity.

You can mist the cage with a hand-held misting bottle, a pressurized unit or an automated misting system. An inexpensive hand-held misting bottle usually suffices for those caring for a single pet lizard, while those maintaining several individuals often find the latter two options more efficient.

You can also add water to the substrate or incorporate a large water dish in the enclosure to raise the humidity level.

Whichever method you choose to raise the enclosure humidity, be sure to monitor the humidity levels with a quality hygrometer, rather than simply guessing at the humidity level.

Most tegus will likely thrive with a relative humidity in the 60 to 80 percent range, although they can probably tolerate slightly lower humidity levels, provided they are provided with access to ample water and damp hiding places.

Chapter 13: Interacting with Your Tegu

Although tegus will never be confused with bearded dragons or other "lap lizards," most eventually learn to tolerate interaction with their keeper. Captive bred individuals are far more likely to become tame than wild caught individuals are.

Some keepers feel that some tegu species – notably *Salvator merianae* – are tamer than others are, but this is hard to establish empirically.

Handling Your Tegu

The very best way to handle your tegu is to allow him to walk on your outstretched hands and forearms, rather than physically restraining him. However, you may need to grip him gently, if you need to examine him closely.

To pick up your tegu, try to slide a finger or hand (if the lizard is large) underneath the lizard's chin. Gently apply upward pressure, and the lizard will usually begin moving up your arm or hand. Keep lifting up gently and the lizard will likely crawl right onto you as though you were a tree.

You may need to help convince your lizard that you are not a threat by hand-feeding him for some time. After doing this for a while, he may be willing to crawl onto your hand voluntarily.

You can allow your tegu to walk around on your hand or just hang out on your arm for 5 or 10 minutes, provided that the lizard does not begin showing signs of stress.

You can just hold him while you tend to minor duties in the cage, but if you must perform substantial maintenance to the habitat, it is wiser to place him in a temporary holding cage while you carry out the necessary tasks.

When it is time to put him back in his enclosure, lower your hand to the floor of his cage and he'll likely walk away on his own.

Always be patient when transferring a tegu to or from your hands. Try to "encourage" rather than "force" movements. Sometimes, tickling a tegu's tail lightly will stimulate it to move more quickly.

In the Event of a Bite

In the event that your lizard bites, try to remain calm. Bites from small tegus generally cause nothing more than a small break in the skin. However, while the bite of a young tegu can be described as a strong pinch, the bite of a mature adult is indeed quite powerful. A bite from a large individual can lead to much more substantial injuries.

The first thing to do in the case of a bite is to immobilize the lizard so he cannot thrash his head from side to side. If you can move him back into his cage, you may be able to get him to flee by simply releasing him.

If this does not work, you can try to place the lizard into a tub of cool water. If nothing else works, you will have to try to pry his mouth open – a soft spatula makes a great tool for doing so, as you can slip it into the lizard's mouth with some force, yet the flexibility of the tool will prevent serious injury to his gums or teeth.

Wash all bites with soap and warm water, and consult your doctor if the bite breaks the skin.

Transporting Your Pet

Although you should strive to avoid any unnecessary travel with your tegu, circumstances often demand that you do (such as when your lizard becomes ill).

Strive to make the journey as stress-free as possible for your pet. This means protecting him from physical harm, as well as blocking as much stressful stimuli as possible.

The best type of container to use when transporting your lizard is a plastic storage box. Add several ventilation holes to plastic containers to provide suitable ventilation.

Add a few paper towel tubes to the container so your lizard can hide and feel secure while traveling. Place a few paper towels or some clean newspaper in the bottom of the box to absorb any fluids, should your lizard defecate or discharge urates.

Monitor your lizard regularly, but avoid constantly opening the container to take a peak. Checking up on your pet once every half-hour or so is more than sufficient.

Pay special attention to the enclosure temperatures while traveling. Use your digital thermometer to monitor the air temperatures inside the transportation container. Try to keep the temperatures in the high-70s Fahrenheit (25 to 26 degrees Celsius) so that your pet will remain comfortable. Use the air-conditioning or heater in your vehicle as needed to keep the animal within this range.

Keep your tegu's transportation container as stable as possible while traveling. Do not jostle your pet unnecessarily and always use a gentle touch when moving the container. Never leave the container unattended.

Because you cannot control the thermal environment, it is not wise to take your lizard with you on public transportation.

Hygiene

Reptiles can carry *Salmonella* spp., *Escherichia coli* and several other zoonotic pathogens. Accordingly, it is imperative that you use good hygiene practices when handling reptiles.

Always wash your hands with soap and warm water each time you touch your pet, his habitat or the tools you use to care for him. Antibacterial soaps are preferred, but standard hand soap will suffice.

In addition to keeping your hands clean, you must also take steps to ensure your environment does not become contaminated with pathogens. In general, this means keeping your lizard and any of the tools and equipment you use to maintain his habitat separated from your belongings.

Establish a safe place for preparing his food, storing equipment and cleaning his habitat. Make sure these places are far from the places in which you prepare your food and personal effects. Never wash cages or tools in kitchens or bathrooms that are used by humans.

Always clean and sterilize any items that become contaminated by the germs from your lizard or his habitat.

Chapter 14: Common Health Concerns

Your lizard cannot tell you when he is sick; like most other reptiles, tegus endure illness stoically. This does not mean that injuries and illnesses do not cause them distress, but without expressive facial features, they do not *look* like they are suffering.

In fact, reptiles typically do not display symptoms until the disease has already reached an advanced state. Accordingly, it is important to treat injuries and illnesses promptly – often with the help of a qualified veterinarian –in order to provide your pet with the best chance of recovery.

Finding a Suitable Veterinarian
Tegu keepers often find that it is more difficult to find a veterinarian to treat their lizard than it is to find a vet to treat a cat or dog. Relatively few veterinarians treat reptiles, so it is important to find a reptile-oriented vet *before* you need one. There are a number of ways to do this:

- You can search veterinarian databases to find one that is local and treats reptiles.

- You can inquire with your dog or cat vet to see if he or she knows a qualified reptile-oriented veterinarian to whom he or she can refer you.

- You can contact a local reptile-enthusiast group or club. Most such organizations will be familiar with the local veterinarians.

- You can inquire with local nature preserves or zoos. Most will have relationships with veterinarians that treat reptiles and other exotic animals.

Those living in major metropolitan areas may find a vet reasonably close, but rural reptile keepers may have to travel considerable distances to find veterinary assistance.

If you do not have a reptile-oriented veterinarian within driving distance, you can try to find a conventional veterinarian who is willing to consult with a reptile-oriented veterinarian via the phone or internet. These types of "two-for-one" visits may be expensive, as you will have to pay for both the actual visit and the consultation, but they may be your only option.

Reasons to Visit the Veterinarian

While reptiles do not require vaccinations or similar routine treatments, they may require visits to treat illnesses or injuries. However, you needn't travel to the vet every time your tegu refuses a meal or experiences a bad shed. In fact, unnecessary veterinary visits may prove more harmful than helpful, so it is important to distinguish between those ailments that require care and those that are best treated at home.

When in doubt, contact your veterinarian and solicit his or her advice before packing up your lizard and hauling him in for an office visit. However, any of the following signs or symptoms can indicate serious problems, and each requires veterinary evaluation.

Visit your veterinarian when:

- Anytime your lizard wheezes, exhibits labored breathing or produces a mucus discharge from its nostrils or mouth.

- Your lizard produces soft or watery feces for longer than 48 hours.

- He suffers any significant injury. Common examples include thermal burns, friction damage to the rostral (nose) region or injured feet.

- Reproductive issues occur, such as being unable to deliver eggs. If a lizard appears nervous, agitated or otherwise stressed and unable to expel eggs, see your veterinarian immediately.

- Your lizard fails to feed for an extended period (more than three or four days and not associated with seasonal or reproductive changes).

- Your lizard displays any unusual lumps, bumps or lesions.

- Your lizard's intestines prolapse.

Ultimately, you must make all the decisions on behalf of your lizard, so weigh the pros and cons of each veterinary trip carefully and make the best decision you can for your pet. Just be sure that you always strive to act in his best interest.

Common Health Problems

The following are a few of the most common health problems that afflict tegus. Their causes and the suggested course of action are also discussed.

Retained or Poor Sheds

Tegus do not shed their entire skin at one time, as snakes do. Instead, they tend to shed in numerous pieces, over several hours or days. Occasionally, this can cause them to retain portions of their old skin. While this is not usually a big problem, care must be taken to ensure that the face, tail tip and toes all shed completely. If skin is retained in these places, blood flow can be restricted, eventually causing the death of the associated tissues. Sometimes this leads to the loss of toes or tail tips.

The best way to remove retained sheds is by temporarily increasing the enclosure humidity and misting your animal more frequently. In cases involving small amounts of retained skin, this may be enough to resolve the problem within a few days.

If this does not work, you may need to remove the retained skin manually. If the skin is partially free, you can try to get a grip on the loose part and gently pull the remaining skin enough to remove it (do not try this if the retained skin attaches near the eyes).

If the retained skin is not peeling up around the edges, you will not be able to grip it. In such cases, use a damp paper towel to gently rub the area in question. With a little bit of water and gentle friction, you can usually dislodge the retained skin.

Always avoid forcing the skin off, as you may injure your pet. If the skin does not come off easily, return him to his cage and try again in 12 to 24 hours. Usually, repeated dampening will loosen the skin sufficiently to be removed.

If repeated treatments do not yield results, consult your veterinarian. He may feel that the retained shed is not causing a problem, and advise you to leave it attached – it should come off with the next shed. Alternatively, it if is causing a problem, the veterinarian can remove it without much risk of harming your pet.

Respiratory Infections
Like humans, lizards can suffer from respiratory infections. Tegus with respiratory infections exhibit fluid or mucus draining from their nose and/or mouth, may be lethargic and are unlikely to eat. They may also spend excessive amounts of time basking on or under the heat source, in an effort to induce a "behavioral fever."

Bacteria, or, less frequently, fungi or parasites often cause respiratory infections. In addition, cleaning products, perfumes, pet dander and other particulate matter can irritate a reptile's respiratory tract as well. Some such bacteria and most fungi are ubiquitous, and only become problematic when they overwhelm an animal's immune system. Other bacteria and most viruses are transmitted from one lizard to another.

To reduce the chances of illnesses, keep your lizard separated from other lizards, keep his enclosure exceptionally clean and be sure to provide the best husbandry possible, in terms of temperature, ventilation and humidity. Additionally, avoid stressing your pet by handling him too frequently, or exposing him to chaotic situations.

Veterinary care is almost always required to treat respiratory infections. Your vet will likely take samples of the mucus and have it analyzed to determine the causal agent. The veterinarian will then prescribe medications, if appropriate, such as antibiotics.

It is imperative to carry out the actions prescribed by your veterinarian exactly as stated, and keep your lizard's stress level very low while he is healing. Stress can reduce immune function, so avoid handling him unnecessarily, and consider covering the front of his cage while he recovers.

"Mouth Rot"
Mouth rot – properly called stomatitis – is identified by noting discoloration, discharge or cheesy-looking material in your tegu's mouth. Mouth rot can be a serious illness, and requires the attention of your veterinarian.

While mouth rot can follow an injury (such as happens when a lizard rubs his snout against the sides of the cage) it can also arise from systemic illness. Your veterinarian will cleanse your lizard's mouth and potentially prescribe an antibiotic.

Your veterinarian may recommend withholding food until the problem is remedied. Always be sure that lizards recovering from mouth rot have immaculately clean habitats, with appropriate humidity and ventilation, as well as ideal temperatures.

Internal Parasites

In the wild, most tegus carry some internal parasites. While it may not be possible to keep a reptile completely free of internal parasites, it is important to keep these levels in check.

Consider any wild-caught animals to be parasitized until proven otherwise. While most captive bred tegus should have relatively few internal parasites, they are not immune to them.

Preventing parasites from building to pathogenic levels requires strict hygiene. Many parasites build up to dangerous levels when lizards are kept in cages that are continuously contaminated from feces.

Most internal parasites that are of importance for lizards are transmitted via the fecal-oral route. This means that eggs (or a similar life stage) of the parasites are released with the feces. If the lizard inadvertently ingests these, the parasites can develop inside his body and cause increased problems.

Parasite eggs are usually microscopic and easily carried by gentle drafts, where they may stick to cage walls or land in the feeding dish. Later, when the tegu snaps up an insect, he ingests the eggs as well.

Internal parasites may cause your lizard to vomit, pass loose stools, fail to grow or refuse food entirely. Other parasites may produce no obvious symptoms at all, despite causing considerable damage to your pet's internal organs. This illustrates the importance of routine fecal examinations (which do not necessarily require that you bring your pet into the office).

Your veterinarian will usually examine your pet's feces if he suspects internal parasites. By looking at the type of eggs inside the feces, your veterinarian can prescribe an appropriate medication. Many parasites are easily treated with anti-parasitic medications, but often, these medications must be given several times to eradicate the pathogens completely.

Some parasites may be transmissible to people, so always take proper precautions, including regular hand washing and keeping reptiles and their cages away from kitchens and other areas where foods are prepared.

Examples of common internal parasites include roundworms, tapeworms and amoebas.

External Parasites
Tegus can theoretically suffer from external parasites, such as ticks and mites, but this appears to be a relatively rare occurrence.

Ticks should be removed manually. Using tweezers grasp the tick as close as possible to the lizard's skin and pull with steady, gentle pressure. Do not place anything over the tick first, such as petroleum jelly, or carry out any other "home remedies," such as burning the tick with a match. Such techniques may cause the tick to inject more saliva (which may contain diseases or bacteria) into the tegu's body.

Drop the tick in a jar of isopropyl alcohol to kill it. It is a good idea to bring these to your veterinarian for analysis. Do not contact ticks with your bare hands, as many species can transmit disease to humans.

Mites are another matter entirely. While ticks are generally large enough to see easily, mites are about the size of a pepper flake. Whereas tick infestations usually only tally a few individuals, mite infestations may include thousands of individual parasites.

Mites may afflict wild caught lizards, but, as they are not confined to a small cage, such infestations are usually self-limiting. However, in captivity, mite infestations can approach plague proportions.

After a female mite feeds on a lizard, she drops off and finds a safe place (such as a tiny crack in a cage or among the substrate) to deposit her eggs. After the eggs hatch, they travel back to your pet (or to other lizards in your collection) where they feed and perpetuate the lifecycle.

Whereas a few mites may represent little more than an inconvenience to the lizard, a significant infection stresses them considerably, and may even cause death through anemia. This is particularly true for small or young animals. Additionally, mites may transmit disease from one animal to another.

There are a number of different methods for eradicating a mite infestation. In each case, there are two primary steps that must be taken: You must eradicate the lizard's parasites as well as the parasites in the environment (which includes the room in which the cage resides).

Soaking is often an effective strategy for ridding a lizard of mites, but it is not a viable option for all lizards. In some cases a chemical treatment will be necessary. Consult with your veterinarian, who can recommend a prudent treatment.

You will also need to perform a thorough cage cleaning to eliminate the problem. To do so, you must remove everything from the cage, including water dishes, substrates and cage props. Sterilize all impermeable cage items, and discard the substrate and all porous cage props – including plants and trees. Vacuum the area around the cage and wipe down all of the nearby surfaces with a wet cloth.

It may be necessary to repeat this process several times to eradicate the mites completely. Accordingly, the very best strategy is to avoid contracting mites in the first place. This is why it is important to purchase your tegu from a reliable breeder or retailer, and keep him quarantined from potential mite vectors.

Long-Term Anorexia
While tegus may refuse the occasional meal, they should not fast for prolonged periods of time.

The most common reasons that tegus refuse food are improper temperatures and illness. Parasites and bacterial infections can also cause lizards to refuse food. Consult your veterinarian anytime that your pet refuses food for longer than three or four days.

Chapter 15: Breeding Tegus

Tegus often breed readily and they are a great option for those who'd like to try their hand at captive reproduction. However, there is certainly no reason you must breed them, unless you want to. Just be sure you are ready to provide the proper care for both the adults and the ensuing offspring before setting out to breed them.

Sexing Tegus

Obviously, you must have at a sexual pair of animals to produce viable eggs and eventual offspring. While it is sometimes easy to identify mature male tegus based on their large size and the presence of jowls, most tegus offer few external clues about their sex.

Accordingly, it is often necessary to probe the animals, once they've reached maturity to verify their sex. You'll want your vet or an experienced keeper to probe them for you, so you do not injure your animals in the process.

To probe a tegu, a smooth, lubricated stainless steel shaft is inserted into the animal's cloaca. If the animal is a male, the probe will pass into one of the inverted hemipenes, which will allow it to penetrate relatively far. By contrast, because females lack hemipenes, the probe will not travel very far into their tail section.

It is usually wise to probe both sides of an animal's vent, just to be sure you have correctly identified its sex.

Note the jowls on this mature male red tegu.

Pre-Breeding Conditioning

Breeding reptiles always entails risk, so it is wise to refrain from breeding any animals that are not in excellent health. Breeding is especially stressful for female tegus, who must withstand potential injuries during mating, and produce numerous, nutrient-rich eggs.

Animals slated for breeding trials must have excellent body weight, but obesity is to be avoided, as it is associated with reproductive problems. Ensure that the lizards are appropriately hydrated, and are free of parasites, infections and injuries.

Additionally, it is important that any females slated for breeding programs have adequate calcium stores.

Cycling

Cycling is the terms used to describe the climactic changes keepers impose upon their animals, which seek to mimic the natural seasonal changes in an animal's natural habitat.

For tegus, this typically means providing them with a cool "winter" period that lasts 3 to 5 months. You'll need to withhold food during this time (as well as for the entire week before subjecting them to the cool temperatures), but be sure that water remains available at all times.

After the cooling period is over, you can restore the proper temperatures and begin offering food again.

Pairing

Once your tegus have completed their brumation, it is time to begin introducing the male to the female. Note that tegus typically breed most successfully in 1:1 ratios, but it is possible to house one male with several females, if the cage is suitably large. Males shouldn't be housed together unless you are using room-sized enclosures.

Use care when making introductions, as males are sometimes overly aggressive when attempting to mate. Remove the male from his enclosure, and gently place him inside the female's cage.

You can leave the male with the female, but check on them periodically to ensure the pair are not antagonistic toward each other. Try not to disturb the lizards any more than necessary during the process.

Copulation may begin almost immediately, or it may take several hours to occur. The pair may copulate only once, or they may copulate several times over many days. It is usually wise to house the pair together for several days, to allow for multiple copulations, thereby helping to ensure good fertility.

After successful mating, the female will begin constructing a nest under her substrate or some form of cover. Once this occurs, it is wise to consider her gravid. Remove the male at this time and begin handling her only when necessary.

Gravid females often become highly protective of their nest, so do not be alarmed if your normally tame pet becomes quite willing to bite during this time.

Egg Deposition and Incubation

About a week after finishing the nest, most females will begin depositing eggs. You'll need to remove the female gently (it is a good idea to allow her to soak for about an hour at this point in time), and then remove the eggs. You'll then need to place them in an incubator.

Place the eggs in deli cups or plastic food containers, half-filled with slightly dampened vermiculite (most keepers use a 1:1 ratio of vermiculite to water, by weight) -- it should clump when compressed, but not release any water.

Avoid rotating the eggs while removing and transferring them to the egg chamber. Bury the eggs halfway into the vermiculite and close the container.

You can purchase a commercially produced incubator or you can construct your own. Most any incubator designed for use with reptile eggs will suffice, but it is wise to test the unit and ensure it holds consistent temperatures before you are faced with eggs.

You can make your own incubator by filling a 10-gallon aquarium with a few inches of water. Place an aquarium heater in the water, and set the thermostat at the desired temperature. Place a brick in the water and rest the egg chamber on top of the brick. Cover the aquarium with a glass top to keep the heat and moisture contained.

Most eggs will hatch in about 60 days, when incubated between 86 to 90 degrees Fahrenheit (30 to 32 degrees Celsius). Humidity levels of about 90 percent are usually sufficient for proper development. As with all other aspects of tegu care, the various species exhibit slightly different needs and tendencies, so you may have to adjust your procedures accordingly.

Neonatal Husbandry

Once the young begin hatching from their eggs, you can remove them from the incubator or parental cage and place them in a small cage or "nursery."

A scaled-down version of an adult habitat, such as a small plastic storage box, makes a satisfactory nursery. Place several pieces of crumpled paper, commercial hides or plant clippings to provide the young with some form of cover.

Mist the young several times per day and keep the temperatures between about 80 and 86 degrees Fahrenheit (26 and 30 degrees Celsius). You can initiate feeding trials within a day or two, but most will not begin to feed until after their first shed.

Keep the young in the nursery until they begin feeding regularly. At this point, you can begin breaking them into small groups and placing them in individual enclosures.

Chapter 16: Further Reading

Never stop learning more about your new pet's natural history, biology and captive care. This is the only way to ensure that you are providing your new tegu with the highest quality of life possible.

It's always more fun to watch your lizard than read about him, but by accumulating more knowledge, you'll be better able to provide him with a high quality of life.

Books
Bookstores and online book retailers offer a treasure trove of information that will advance your quest for knowledge. While books represent an additional cost involved in reptile care, you can consider it an investment in your pet's well-being. Your local library may also carry some books about tegus, which you can borrow for no charge.

University libraries are a great place for finding old, obscure or academically oriented books about tegus. You may not be allowed to borrow these books if you are not a student, but you can view and read them at the library.

Herpetology: An Introductory Biology of Amphibians and Reptiles
By Laurie J. Vitt, Janalee P. Caldwell
Top of Form
Bottom of Form
Academic Press, 2013

Understanding Reptile Parasites: A Basic Manual for Herpetoculturists & Veterinarians
By Roger Klingenberg D.V.M.
Advanced Vivarium Systems, 1997

Infectious Diseases and Pathology of Reptiles: Color Atlas and Text
Elliott Jacobson
CRC Press

Designer Reptiles and Amphibians
Richard D. Bartlett, Patricia Bartlett
Barron's Educational Series

Lizards: Windows to the Evolution of Diversity
By Eric R. Pianka, Laurie J. Vit
University of California Press

Magazines

Because magazines are typically published monthly or bi-monthly, they occasionally offer more up-to-date information than books do. Magazine articles are obviously not as comprehensive as books typically are, but they still have considerable value.

Reptiles Magazine
www.reptilesmagazine.com/
Covering reptiles commonly kept in captivity.

Practical Reptile Keeping
http://www.practicalreptilekeeping.co.uk/
Practical Reptile Keeping is a popular publication aimed at beginning and advanced hobbies. Topics include the care and maintenance of popular reptiles as well as information on wild reptiles.

Websites

The internet has made it much easier to find information about reptiles than it has ever been.

However, you must use discretion when deciding which websites to trust. While knowledgeable breeders, keepers and academics operate some websites, many who maintain reptile-oriented websites lack the same dedication to scientific rigor.

Anyone with a computer and internet connection can launch a website and say virtually anything they want about tegus. Accordingly, as with all other research, consider the source of the information before making any husbandry decisions.

The Reptile Report

www.thereptilereport.com/
The Reptile Report is a news-aggregating website that accumulates interesting stories and features about reptiles from around the world.

Kingsnake.com
www.kingsnake.com
After starting as a small website for gray-banded kingsnake enthusiasts, Kingsnake.com has become one of the largest reptile-oriented portals in the hobby. The site features classified advertisements, a breeder directory, message forums and other resources.

The Vivarium and Aquarium News
www.vivariumnews.com/
The online version of the former print publication, The Vivarium and Aquarium News provides in-depth coverage of different reptiles and amphibians in a captive and wild context.

Journals

Journals are the primary place professional scientists turn when they need to learn about tegus. While they may not make light reading, hobbyists stand to learn a great deal from journals.

Herpetologica
www.hljournals.org/
Published by The Herpetologists' League, Herpetologica, and its companion publication, Herpetological Monographs cover all aspects of reptile and amphibian research.

Journal of Herpetology
www.ssarherps.org/
Produced by the Society for the Study of Reptiles and Amphibians, the Journal of Herpetology is a peer-reviewed publication covering a variety of reptile-related topics.

Copeia
www.asihcopeiaonline.org/

Copeia is published by the American Society of Ichthyologists and Herpetologists. A peer-reviewed journal, Copeia covers all aspects of the biology of reptiles, amphibians and fish.

Nature
www.nature.com/

Although Nature covers all aspects of the natural world, many issues contain information that lizard enthusiasts are sure to find interesting.

Supplies

You can obtain most of what you need to maintain tegus through your local pet store, big-box retailer or hardware store, but online retailers offer another option.

Just be sure that you consider the shipping costs for any purchase, to ensure you aren't "saving" yourself a few dollars on the product, yet spending several more dollars to get the product delivered.

Big Apple Pet Supply
http://www.bigappleherp.com

Big Apple Pet Supply carries most common husbandry equipment, including heating devices, water dishes and substrates.

LLLReptile
http://www.lllreptile.com

LLL Reptile carries a wide variety of husbandry tools, heating devices, lighting products and more.

Doctors Foster and Smith
http://www.drsfostersmith.com

Foster and Smith is a veterinarian-owned retailer that supplies husbandry-related items to pet keepers.

Support Organizations

Sometimes, the best way to learn about tegus is to reach out to other keepers and breeders. Check out these organizations, and search for others in your geographic area.

The National Reptile & Amphibian Advisory Council
http://www.nraac.org/
The National Reptile & Amphibian Advisory Council seeks to educate the hobbyists, legislators and the public about reptile and amphibian related issues.

American Veterinary Medical Association
www.avma.org
The AVMA is a good place for Americans to turn if you are having trouble finding a suitable reptile veterinarian.

The World Veterinary Association
http://www.worldvet.org/
The World Veterinary Association is a good resource for finding suitable reptile veterinarians worldwide.

References

Abigail S. Tucker a, G. J. (2014). Evolution and developmental diversity of tooth regeneration. *Seminars in Cell & Developmental Biology*.

Anderson, S. P. (2003). The Phylogenetic Definition of Reptilia. *Systematic Biology*.

Glenn J. Tattersall, C. A. (2016). Seasonal reproductive endothermy in tegu lizards. *ECOLOGY*.

John C. Murphy, M. J. (2016). Cryptic, Sympatric Diversity in Tegu Lizards of the Tupinambis teguixin Group (Squamata, Sauria, Teiidae) and the Description of Three New Species. *PLOS One*.

K. Megan Sheffield, M. T. (2011). Locomotor loading mechanics in the hindlimbs of tegu lizards (Tupinambis merianae): comparative and evolutionary implications. *The Journal of Experimental Biology*.

LEE A. FITZGERALD, J. A. (1999). Molecular Phylogenetics and Conservation of Tupinambis (Sauria: Teiidae). *Copeia*.

Oldrich Zahradnicek, M. B. (2014). The development of complex tooth shape in reptiles. *Frontiers in Physiology*.

Vitor A. Campos, F. H. (2011). First state record and distribution extension of Tupinambis duseni Lönnberg, 1910 (Squamata: Sauria: Teiidae) from Mato Grosso state, central Brazil. *Herpetology Notes*.

Index

Anorexia, 87
Aquariums, 38
Bleach, 66
Breeding, 68
bulbs, 52, 53, 54
cage, 30, 37, 41, 44, 45, 46, 84, 85, 86, 87
Cleaning, 63, 64
CRI, 52, 54
Cypress Mulch, 56, 58
Dimensions, 37
enclosures, 54
Feeding, 67
Gender, 68
habitats, 54
Heat, 28, 42, 43, 44, 45
Heat Cables, 45
Heat Pads, 44
Heat Tape, 45
Heating, 46
Homemade Cages, 39
Hot Rocks, 46
husbandry, 93, 95
Husbandry, 91

lighting, 52, 53
Lights, 51
mites, 86, 87
Mouth rot, 84
Newspaper, 58
online, 92
Orchid Bark, 56
probe, 47
Rheostats, 47
Substrate, 55, 58
temperature, 53
Temperature, 40
Temperatures, 47
Thermal Gradients, 41
Thermometers, 47
Thermostats, 47
trough, 51
ultraviolet radiation, 54
UV, 51, 53
veterinarian, 35, 40, 66, 81, 82, 83, 84, 85, 86, 95, 96
veterinarian's, 40
Water, 28

www.ingramcontent.com/pod-product-compliance
Lightning Source LLC
Chambersburg PA
CBHW060847050426
42453CB00008B/876